Stoicism 101

Kendrick Chambers

© Copyright 2019 - All rights reserved.

The contents of this book may not be reproduced, duplicated or transmitted without direct written permission from the author.

Under no circumstances will any legal responsibility or blame be held against the publisher for any reparation, damages, or monetary loss due to the information herein, either directly or indirectly.

Legal Notice:

This book is copyright protected. This is only for personal use. You cannot amend, distribute, sell, use, quote or paraphrase any part or the content within this book without the consent of the author.

Disclaimer Notice:

Please note the information contained within this document is for educational and entertainment purposes only. Every attempt has been made to provide accurate, up to date and reliable complete information. No warranties of any kind are expressed or implied. Readers acknowledge that the author is not engaging in the rendering of legal, financial, medical or professional advice. The content of this book has been derived from various sources. Please consult a licensed professional before attempting any techniques outlined in this book.

By reading this document, the reader agrees that under no circumstances is the author responsible for any losses, direct or indirect, which are incurred as a result of the use of information contained within this document, including, but not limited to, —errors, omissions, or inaccuracies.

Table of Contents

Introduction 1

Chapter 1: What Is Stoicism? 7

The History Of Stoicism 9

The Cardinal Virtues Of Stoicism 15

Important Beliefs And Principles Of Stoicism 20

Stoics Beliefs For The Modern World 29

Impact Of Stoicism In The Modern World 38

Chapter 2: Stoic Philosophers 101 41

Zeno Of Citium (332–262 BC) 42

Aristo Of Chios (C. 260 BC) 44

Herillus Of Carthage (C. 3rd Century BC) 45

Cleanthes Of Assos (330–232 BC) 46

Chrysippus (C. 280–204 BC) 49

Diogenes Of Babylon (230–150 BC) 50

Antipater Of Tarsus (210–129 BC) 51

Panaetius Of Rhodes (185–109 BC) 52

Posidonius Of Apameia (C. 135 BC – 51 BC) 55

Hecato Of Rhodes (C, 100 BC) 56

Cato The Younger (94–46 BC) 57

Seneca The Younger (4 BC – AD 65) 58

Gaius Musonius Rufus (1st Century AD) 60

Publius Clodius Thrasea Paetus (1st Century AD) 62

Epictetus (AD 55–135) 62

Hierocles (2nd Century AD) 64

Marcus Aurelius (AD 121–180) 65

Chapter 3: Epicureanism Vs. Stoicism 68

What Is Epicureanism? 71

Who Are The Epicureans? 77

Top Quotations Of Epicureanism That Have Withstood The Test Of Time 78

Differences Between Stoicism And Epicureanism 79

Chapter 4: Psychology & Mindset Mastery 85

Self-Awareness And Stoicism 85

Stoics Vs. Non-Stoics 94

How To Develop A Stoic Mindset? 98

Stoic Exercises And Practices For Everyday Life 104

Building Mindfulness With Stoic Affirmations And Meditations 109

Chapter 5: Develop Unbreakable Emotional Intelligence 116

Emotional Intelligence 117

Dealing With Emotions Stoically 118

The Stoic Triangle Of Happiness 121

Negative Visualization 128

Stoic Exercises To Build Self-Awareness And Mindfulness 132

Chapter 6: The Preparation You Need For Modern Day Life 140

Identify Your Inner Control Center 140

Time Is Precious 143

Your Happiness Is Your Responsibility 144

Be Wary Of Distractions 146

Eliminate Vanity And Ego From Your Life 147

Stand Firm On Your Principles 149

Nothing In The World Is Permanent 150

Create Disruptions In Your Life 151

You Always Have A Choice 155

Always Look Inwards 155

Avoid Fear And Paranoia 158

Chapter 7: Introducing A Daily Stoic Routine. 160

Morning Stoic Ritual 160

Meditation.. 163

Mindfulness.. 166

Daily Stoic Affirmations And Quotes For Self-Reflection 172

The Power Of A Stoic Diary............................. 175

Conclusion... 181

Resources 185

Introduction

There is a big misconception about Stoicism today. In modern language, the word 'stoic' is used to refer to an individual who is unemotional and indifferent to pleasure and pain. Well, this concept is nowhere close to the philosophical roots of Stoicism, which is a way of life created and designed by the wise men during the ancient times. Fortunately for us, Stoicism is slowly but surely being revived to enable the modern world to reap its multiple benefits.

In the modern world, we are surrounded by the best conveniences and amenities that we human beings have ever had access to. And yet, so many of us are unhappy and continually searching for ways to be happy and to lead a meaningful life. So, how can Stoicism help you live a happy, meaningful life in today's stress-filled times?

Let me tell you my story and how Stoicism helped me overcome my life battles and continues to do so every day. I work a 9-5 job, which invariably stretches by a couple of hours on a daily basis. With a family including kids and old people to cater to at home, my life was a fertile ground for chaos, confusion, stress, and anguish.

The forest of negative emotions grew so dense and deep in my life that I lost my own self in its darkness. I floundered and struggled to keep sanity around me, and seemed to fail more often than succeed. I seemed to reach my tether's end sooner than later, losing my temper so often that my friends and family chose to keep away from me as much as possible.

Thanks to the unfavorable external conditions of my life, my professional life also was in tatters, as I was not mentally and emotionally strong enough to handle the responsibilities of promotions. So, my boss always found a reason not to promote me even if I had done a great job right through the year. Forget promotions, even small increments and little bonuses were left out of my kitty! It was a bad scene.

I was at my lowest point in life, and when I thought I couldn't fall further down is when I was diagnosed with three serious health problems, namely diabetes Type 2, hypertension, and high cholesterol. That's it! My life was spinning out of control. It was my doctor who encouraged me to look towards Stoicism for help. He told me that drugs and medicines by themselves do far less than our minds if we only choose the right path and stick to it.

He gave me a basic introduction of this ancient way of life and told me to look it up. I came home and spent a lot of time researching on Stoicism during which time I realized that our ancestors were far, far wiser than we can ever become. They knew the perils of excessive greed and desires. Our ancestors didn't need to experience the pain of excesses to realize they need to cut down and moderate desires.

Thanks to the convenience of our modern life, we have forgotten to align ourselves with nature and reason. If a neighbor or colleague has got himself a swanky car, then our desire to match, or better, his acquisition gets so deep that we don't even realize we are falling into a bottomless pit.

The purpose of Stoicism is to help you free yourself from desires and passions because they are the cause of our anguish and suffering. Stoics use reason and apathy to help us achieve this purpose. Apathy, in ancient times, was meant to perceive everything objectively and with clear judgment.

Stoicism teaches you to have a 'passive' response to external stimuli because maintaining equanimity in 'good' and 'bad' experiences depends on our reactions and behaviors and not on the external stimuli. So, the basis of stoicism is to leverage your own ability for self-control and self-discipline to lead a stress-free, happy, and joyful life.

Learning and practicing Stoicism helped me in many ways, including the following:

I realized that all emotions and passions are internal to us. They come from within. If we realize this powerful truth, then it is possible to fight off the negative impacts of these crushing emotions and manage them better than before.

I learned that honesty is truly the best way to lead a stress-free, fulfilling life. Trying to fill your life with facades and pretensions simply adds to anxiety and stress as much as trying to be someone else because you think you are not good enough.

Instead, embracing authenticity and being my own self helped me gain self-respect, which in turn earned me others' respect. Brutal honesty became the cornerstone of the positive change in my life.

One of the biggest causes for worry in my pre-stoic life was fear of failure. I was such a scared person that I couldn't bring myself to take up new challenges. When I realized this aspect of my personality, I could easily understand my boss' decision when she chose to overlook me for promotions.

Stoicism taught me that there was life even after failures. I learned to look at failures as learning opportunities, which made me embrace them instead of running away from them. In fact, today, after learning and practicing stoic principles for over five years, I realize that challenges goad me on to move forward instead of pushing me away!

I learned to live in the moment. Stoicism taught me that most of my fears and anxieties were based on some thoughts related to my future or past life. I was so caught up regretting my past and worrying about my future that I had forgotten the present moment, which is the only thing under my control. Stoicism taught me valuable lessons on how to live 'in the moment' and experience and engage with life fully.

Now my life has really turned around. I am more in control of it than ever before. Additionally, I have learned to realize that life battles are never going to end. Daily battles should not stop you from living life every day and every moment joyfully and in a fulfilling way. And Stoicism is there to help you! Read on, and find out more about this engaging, practical, and easy-to-implement way of life that has been in existence since ancient times.

Chapter 1
What is Stoicism?

So, what is Stoicism? It is a school of philosophy from the times of the ancient Greeks and Romans. Stoicism is the foundation of many modern western religions and cultures, including Christianity. Also, this ancient school of philosophy is believed to the basis of the formation of multiple modern western ideas and thoughts such as feminism, humanism, and cosmopolitanism.

Socrates, one of the most famous ancient Greek philosophers, asked a pertinent question about human life, 'How can we lead a good life?' Stoicism was one of the schools of philosophies among many others that were founded to answer this crucial question on human life.

Stoicism deals with philosophical tenets and principles designed to help individual practitioners lead an emotionally resilient and meaningful life. The principles of Stoicism help to direct our thoughts and behaviors responsibly in an unpredictable world. As unpredictability is a timeless aspect of human life, learning and practicing stoicism can help you at all times.

Stoicism was designed to help human beings handle emotions and resultant erratic behaviors. Stoics train themselves in the realm of fortitude and self-control, which helps them overcome destructive emotions. Stoics do not believe that emotions can be eliminated completely. They only try to minimize the irrational and negative impacts of erratic human feelings through self-control and self-discipline.

Stoics believe in voluntarily abstaining from worldly pleasures to embrace asceticism in order to live a meaningful, happy life in the practical world. Asceticism does not translate to sacrificing everything to live in the forest. Stoics use voluntary abstinence to develop inner peace, clear judgment, and freedom from sufferings caused by undue and unreasonable desires and fears.

It is important to note that Stoicism is not a religion or a set of ethics. Stoicism is a way of life that calls for continuous training and practice. Stoicism involves the use of logic, self-dialogue, and conversations with other practitioners, pondering on the concept of death, and training your mind to focus on the present moment, which can be referred to as mindfulness.

The most important aspect of Stoicism lies in the theory that human beings must align their lives with the Divine Reason of the Universe. The Stoic philosophy is based on the fact that we have little or no control over the external aspects of our lives, whereas we have some amount of control over our own minds and own behaviors. Eventually, external circumstances matter a lot less than our responses to any given situation.

The History of Stoicism

Zeno of Citium founded Stoicism around 301 B.C. This school of philosophy was originally called Zenonism before being renamed to Stoicism. The name 'Stoicism' is derived from Stoa Poikile, which translates to 'The Painted Porch.' During the initial days of this school of philosophy, followers and believers gathered together and held debates in the shade Stoa Poikile in Agora, Athens, as they did not have buildings like Aristotle's Lyceum or Plato's Academy, and hence, the name.

Why did the name get changed from Zenonism to Stoicism? There are many theories for this and chief among them are the following two:

- ❖ Maybe, the later followers did not think that the founders were perfectly wise.
- ❖ They did not want Stoicism to become a cult based on any one personality.

And therefore the name was changed to Stoicism. Many times, Stoicism is referred to as simply The Stoa or the philosophy of the porch. The Stoics met and debated in a public place, allowing any interested person to listen in to the discussions and even walk up and participate in the conversations and debates.

The founder Zeno of Citium was a student of Crates of Thebes, a powerful follower of Cynicism. Zeno toned down the extreme harshness in Cynicism and included real-world practicality and moderation into Stoicism.

Considering that Stoicism seemed to have been founded and established on the streets of Athens, it could be right to say that the principles were for the average, common citizens more than for the elite and aristocrats. And yet, Stoicism became an influential philosophical school in the ancient times with followers who came from a wide cross-section of the society ranging from slaves like Epictetus right up to emperors like Marcus Aurelius.

Right from its birth around 300 B.C. until the 2nd century, Stoicism was a highly regarded and popular school of philosophy. It was practiced by the rich and the poor cutting across societal hierarchies. Everyone was drawn to its tenets that taught people how to lead a good life.

Stoicism became one of the most influential schools of philosophy in the ancient Greco-Roman times. This school of philosophy produced many great thinkers and writers including Seneca the Younger, Cato the

Younger, Panaetius of Rhodes, Posidonius, Marcus Aurelius, and Epictetus.

Historians and philosophers categorize the history of Stoicism into three periods, including:

The early Stoa - During the initial phases, Stoicism was seen as a movement that drew people back to nature, considering that it was against all kinds of societal taboos and superstitions.

Zeno was succeeded by Cleanthes of Assos who was followed by Chrysippus of Soli, one of the most influential thinkers in the history of Stoicism, and who was responsible for creating, designing, and molding Stoicism to what it has become today.

He was the one who brought in the concept of a unified and interconnected account of the universe, use of formal logic, natural ethics, and materialistic physics. Although stoicism focused primarily on ethics, the theories of logic were a big draw for philosophers who came later on.

It is important to note here that Stoicism did not come out of nothing. The early Stoics were influenced by multiple schools of philosophies of ancient times. Stoicism borrowed ideas from Socrates, the Cynics, the Skeptics, and the Academics (Plato's school).

The middle Stoa – Stoicism was introduced to Rome during this period, and Cicero, an influential Roman thinker and philosopher, was sympathetic towards the school even though he was not an ardent follower. His writings are one of the major sources of information for the modern historians as only very few writings from the early Stoa period have survived.

The late Stoa – At this stage, Stoicism gained a large following from influential people in Imperial Rome. Famous Stoics like Seneca the Younger, Gaius Musonius Rufus, Marcus Aurelius, and Epictetus were from this period. A significant portion of the writings and works of these people still survive.

However, by the end of the 2nd century, its popularity waned as the society was taken over by Christian thoughts and ideas. And for nearly two millennia after that, Stoicism seemed to have been forgotten by the world. However, many people were influenced by Stoicism even if there was some amount of criticism towards it.

The important historical figures influenced by Stoic principles even after its popularity waned include Thomas Aquinas, early Christian clergy, Thomas More, Giordano Bruno, and others.

Additionally, in the 16th century, a Belgian humanist Justus Lipsius founded a syncretic movement called neo-stoicism combining Stoic and Christian thoughts, ideas, and philosophies. Neo-stoicism encouraged people to lead a good, moral life by not yielding to passions and emotions like greed, sorrow, fear, and joy. Instead, people must simply submit themselves to God.

Thanks to some of the ancient documents that survived the ravages of time, the modern psychology and philosophy scholars were able to revive the interest in Stoicism. The surviving works and writings of Marcus Aurelius, Epictetus, and Seneca, who was an adviser and tutor to Emperor Nero helped in reviving this ancient philosophical system.

The Cardinal Virtues of Stoicism

One of the primary principles of Stoicism is referred to as the Four Cardinal Virtues, which include justice, prudence, temperance, and fortitude. In modern language, these four words could be read as morality (justice), wisdom (prudence), moderation (temperance), and courage (fortitude).

This concept of understanding the four cardinal elements mentioned above is believed to have been in existence from the days of Plato and Socrates, and the Stoics did borrow the idea from the ancient Greek and Roman philosophers. However, the Stoics added new dimensions to the four cardinals of virtue and believed that everything in this world has to be done in harmony with Nature and the Universe. Before we go into what Stoics added to the existing four cardinal virtues, let us look at each of them in a bit of detail from a stoical perspective.

Justice – The Greek word for this virtue is 'dikaiosune' which does not really have a perfect synonym in English. The word 'justice' is too narrow and shallow to include everything that Stoics cover in this cardinal virtue. Justice from a Stoic perspective does not refer only to the legal sense of the word but include everything morality.

Stoics follow the principles of virtue in all their relationships with the people and the world around them.

For example, your sense of piety towards your god or even a mother's love towards her children will have to be encompassed in morality. Morality or justice also includes benevolence, kindness, goodwill towards other people, etc. and other aspects of social justice that Stoics believe in deeply.

Justice refers to the social and moral wisdom that we need to apply to our actions and behaviors with the rest of society. It is the knowledge of the fair distribution of value to everyone in society. The crucial subdivisions of justice included in stoicism are good-heartedness, piety, fair dealing, and public spiritedness.

Prudence – Referred to as phronesis, prudence relates to the use of wisdom in the practical world. Prudence is a vital element of Stoicism and refers to the knowledge of knowing and discerning between the good, the bad, and the indifferent aspects of human life in society.

Prudence is to know, understand, and appreciate the value of all the things in your life, practically and rationally. Prudence is the opposite of ignorance, which is the vice every Stoic strives hard to keep out of his or her life. In this sense, prudence is considered to be the most important virtue of Stoics. The value of prudence or practical wisdom is even connected to the word 'philosophy' which means 'the love of wisdom.'

Some Stoics divide prudence into two parts, namely understanding or *sunesis* and good counsel or *euboulia*. Through this division, Stoics acknowledge the importance of the communication and articulation of values, morals, and principles to other people honestly and tactfully. That means, Stoics gave a lot of importance to the correct form of communication. Also, Stoicism includes the fact that each person should be prudent enough to give himself or herself good counsel as well.

Prudence is further divided into numerous subdivisions, including good calculation, excellent deliberation, quick-wittedness, resourcefulness, a deep sense of purpose, etc.

Moderation –Like justice, moderation or temperance in Stoicism affects multiple aspects of human life, including self-discipline and self-control over one's desires, propriety, and self-awareness. Moderation is the opposite of licentiousness or wantonness, another vice that is anathema to believers of Stoicism.

Moderation consists of the knowledge of what to avoid, embrace, and be indifferent to in your life. This virtue guides our intentions and impulses and teaches you to look at everything in the world and your life objectively and detachedly. Stoics use moderation to overcome their unreasonable desires and fears and free themselves of unhealthy passions and excessive attachment to materialistic things.

The moderation virtue in stoicism includes subdivisions like orderliness, organization skills, self-control, and modesty.

Courage – This virtue in Stoicism includes courage (which is simple to understand) and to endure discomfort and pain. Understandably, courage is the opposite of cowardice. Most Stoics combine this virtue with moderation with the following idea; moderate your desires and have the courage to face your fears.

The fact that moderation and courage are crucial virtues to be mastered means that Stoics believe that even the most ardent follower of Stoicism encounters desires and fears. No human being, no matter how hard he or she tries, can free himself completely from the problems of overcoming desires and fears. Therefore, everyone must work to master the virtues of courage and moderation so that we can continuously battle with desires and fears.

Courage, as per stoicism, teaches you to discern between what is terrible, not terrible, and all other elements in between as well. Courage also refers to 'standing firm' on your principles and enduring challenges and problems through the guidance of wisdom. The subdivisions in the virtue of courage include confidence, endurance, stout-heartedness, great-heartedness, and love of work.

Important Beliefs and Principles of Stoicism

Interestingly, Stoicism and Buddhism, the ancient religion founded in India by Gautama Buddha in around 500 B.C., have a lot in common. One of the most striking similarities between the two philosophical thoughts is the ethical teaching that both offer. Just like the virtues of Stoicism, Buddhism talks of four noble truths, namely:

1. All life is suffering.
2. Desires are the cause of suffering.

3. Happiness can be achieved by eliminating desires.
4. Self-discipline and moral restraint help you eliminate desires from your life.

Also, Stoics strongly believe in aligning themselves to the ways of Nature using the four cardinal virtues, namely justice, prudence, courage, and moderation. Stoics strive to live in harmony with the divine power of the universe and by recognizing and acknowledging the essential value of everyone and everything in this vast universe.

Even in those ancient days, stoicism encouraged egalitarianism and also urged for slaves to be treated as equals. Stoics believed that everyone is a Son of God, which echoes Socrates' proclamation that he is neither a Greek nor an Athenian but a citizen of the world. Stoicism is, perhaps, one of the earliest philosophies to preach and practice equality of all men and denied discrimination based on wealth and social rank.

One of the tenets preached by Seneca the Younger a stoic from the 1st century A.D. is in the realm of anger management. This timeless tenet holds that anger and outbursts of this negative emotion can be controlled by each of us. Seneca the Younger dedicated an entire book to anger management.

He said that anger is caused by having overly unrealistic expectations that end in disappointment. Instead, Seneca the Younger urged people to take a more pessimistic attitude to help us mentally prepare ourselves for bad scenarios, which in turn can help us manage and temper our anger. Other tenets and beliefs of stoic thought include:

Logic and knowledge – Stoics assert the value and importance of knowledge and logic, both of which are attainable through reason and verification. The process of verifying the acquired knowledge can be done through discussions and debates with experts in the relevant field, the collective judgment of all of humankind, and the logical thoughts and ideas that form in our own minds.

Stoicism holds that the human senses are continually receiving and collecting sensations that are passed into our minds and form impressions there. The human mind is capable of discerning between good, bad, and indifferent impressions and can reject or approve the false and true ones, respectively. This particular tenet of Stoicism was in stark contrast to Plato's Idealism, which proposed that everything is sourced in the human mind, and all senses are illusory and erroneous.

The stoic egg – Stoicism has three parts to it, including logic, physics, and ethics with ethics being the most crucial component. Ethics in Stoicism relates to how to live your life in the best way possible. But, living a good, ethical life needs the help of logic (understanding the powers and limitations of human capability) and physics (knowing how the world works). Let us look at these three components in a bit of detail.

As per Stoic physics, the universe began with a primordial or cosmic fire. The entire world is made up of matter, and everything that happens in the world has a cause. The universe is organized based on logical, rational principles or Logos. Some Stoics referred to this phenomenon of Logos as God.

The fact that nature is understandable through observation and rational thought is the primary reason as to why we can scientifically investigate nature and arrive at logical and rational conclusions. One of the most significant outcomes from the physics branch of Stoicism is the belief that we must live in accordance and aligned with nature and the universe

Logic in Stoicism includes the concept of logic as we understand it in modern times, along with epistemology (or the theory of knowledge), rhetoric, psychology, and other social sciences. The system of logic devised and created by the Stoics was an alternative to the one already in existence, which was created by Aristotle. However, Stoic logic remained forgotten until it was rediscovered when propositional logic was invented in the modern world. Propositional logic was already a part of Stoic logic.

Like modern logicians, the ancient Stoics clearly distinguished between abstract and corporeal ideas. For example, they differentiated between material objects and intangible ideas like mathematical concepts. The logic in Stoicism taught them that anyone could learn by observation and reason, which is essential to separating false elements from true elements. Another modernistic and scientific outlook of the ancient Stoics in the realm of logic was the belief that knowledge can be obtained only through discussions and debates with experts of the relevant field.

Stoic ethics is related to practical philosophy and is the most important of the three arms of Stoicism. One of the first misconceptions to discard when it comes to learning stoic ethics is that life has to be led with a stiff upper lip and by suppressing emotions. Stoicism is about redirecting the power of emotions to achieve inner peace and an equanimous attitude towards all life experiences. A Stoic learned to distance himself or herself from the enormous power of emotions like love, anger, grief, etc. This detachment empowered the person to see whether the experienced feelings are appropriate to a given situation or not so that the individual knows if he or she needs to discard or cultivate the emotions.

Stoics understood the importance of correct judgment and learned how to distinguish between eupathos or responding based on correct and objective judgment and propathos or impulsive/instinctive responses. Stoics believe that a good life defined as eudaimonia can be had if one chooses to cultivate good morals based on the four virtues, namely prudence, courage, temperance, and justice.

Another crucial ethical idea behind Stoicism is the ability to distinguish between the preferred and dispreferred elements of life. For example, wealth, prosperity, hierarchical rank, etc. are dispreferred elements of life because they do not contribute to the ethical worth of an individual.

Stoics believe that people can experience eudaimonia regardless of whether they are rich or poor, an emperor or a slave, sick or healthy. Some elements are useful in leading a good life, which are referred to as preferred, and those that come in the way of leading a good life are dispreferred.

Stoics also clearly differentiate between things that are under our control and those that are not. For example, our thoughts, reactions, and responses to external stimuli, attitudes, etc. are under our control, whereas external stimuli and most other aspects of the universe are not under our control.

The trick to being a successful stoic is to focus on what is under your control. This attitude brings about inner peace because effectively, you are letting go of those things that are beyond your control. A true Stoic will not waste his or her time, energy, and other resources on uncontrollable elements of life. Instead, he or she will use these limited resources on controllable things to bring about positive changes and achieve inner peace. Stoics know, understand, and appreciate the fact that there is no sense in dwelling on things that they have no control over.

Metaphysics in Stoicism - Metaphysically speaking, Stoics believe that the universe is a material thing, but it can also reason out and make things happen logically and practically. This power that reasons can be called nature or God is divided into two parts, the active and the passive. The active part of this divine power is described as logos or fate, and it is an intelligent ether or primordial fire that acts on the passive part, which is nothing but matter.

The souls in all living things, including animals and human beings, are emanations of the active part or the primordial fire, and are, therefore, subject to fate. The concept of the primordial fire found in all life is borrowed from Heraclitus who saw the unity and connection amongst everything in the universe. Like Heraclitus, Stoicism holds a cyclical view of the universe and believes that everything that emanates from the fire goes back to fire.

Therefore, Stoics believe that everything, including God and words, is nothing but matter, which is acted upon by the primordial fire. Emotions are also material because they have a physical, tangible manifestation like tears, smiles, frowns, etc. The soul and mind are also material and matter because they produce thoughts and/or impressions of sensations, which results in physical body movements. And this phenomenon would not have been possible if the soul, mind, and body were not all made up of matter.

Stoicism believes that the entire world is one referred to as monism. A divine reality or power pervades the entire universe, and this concept is called pantheism. Therefore, as per Stoicism, the universe is a big living body with multiple parts like the planets, sun, stars, etc.

All the parts of this gigantic universe are interconnected, which means events and experiences in one place are also happening in another place. Also, Stoics are of the belief that everything in the universe is predetermined although human beings have some amount of free will, which we can exercise.

Stoics Beliefs for the Modern World

The following points are Stoic strategies that work extremely well for every human being in the modern world.

Align your life to nature - Eudaimonia is the ultimate goal of a Stoic, which can be achieved only by aligning your life with the ways of nature. Eudaimonia or the good/flourishing life means we should a rational life because human beings are rational animals, unlike wild animals that are not empowered with this critical trait to reason out and think things through before acting.

Nature has given human beings social and mental abilities needed to follow a life based on rational thinking. We must not behave in a beastly, irrational manner because this attitude is against what nature intended for us. Therefore, human beings are meant to use reason, logic, and rational thinking in order to achieve eudaimonia.

Live by the virtues of Stoicism at all times - Use prudence, justice, courage, and temperance to lead a balanced, happy, and fulfilling life. You must practice these virtues in all aspects of your life. For example, if you choose to show courage in front of a weak person and show fear and uncertainty before a strong person, then you are not virtuous. You are manipulative. You must have the nerve to stand up for your beliefs and principles at all times and not only in instances that are suitable for you.

Focus on the controllable elements, and let go of other things - One of the most important lessons that have immense value today is to know and focus on things that are under your control, and let go of everything else. The only part of life you have control over is you and your emotions, judgments, and thoughts. Practically, everything else in this life is beyond your control.

Therefore, when you come across difficult times, focus on what you can do to make things better, and work on them. Stoicism teaches us that blaming the external world not only drives you away from inner peace but also adds to your pain and agony. It is prudent to do what you can do and avoid worrying excessively about things you cannot do.

The fact that only we are responsible for our lives is one of the most empowering elements we can borrow from Stoicism and implement self-motivated behaviors in our daily life.

Discern between the good, the bad, and the indifferent - In Stoicism, good means the four cardinal virtues, and the bad are the opposite of these virtues referred to as vices. Embrace the virtues (which contribute positively to eudaimonia) and discard the vices (contribute negatively to eudaimonia), which include indulgence (opposite of temperance), folly (opposite of wisdom), injustice (opposite of justice), and cowardice (opposite of courage).

Indifferent things include everything else that falls between vices and virtues. For example, fame, reputation, wealth, health, life, death, etc. are all indifferent elements of life because they do not contribute to eudaimonia. Unfortunately, in the modern world, most of us focus on the indifferent aspects of our lives like wealth and fame, and to achieve these indifferent things, we embrace and engage with vices. This attitude drives us increasingly further away from eudaimonia.

It is crucial to remember that indifferent with respect to Stoicism is not about being cold. Indifferent only means that these things have been given to us by a higher power for some specific purpose, and it makes no difference to your ability to achieve eudaimonia whether you have them or not. However, you can love them the same way you love and embrace virtues.

Indifferent means that even when you don't have access to wealth, fame, etc., you can live a meaningful and fulfilling life.

Take action - Stoicism does not preach or practice the perspective of the lazy arguing person. Don't argue for the sake of arguing or avoiding work or action. Of course, you control your actions and responses. However, doing nothing will not get you anywhere. Choose your path and follow it diligently. There is no place for laziness and lethargy in Stoicism. Take action to achieve eudaimonia.

Stoicism does not stop with learning and mastering abstract ideas. On the contrary, it exhorts people to observe, watch, and do the right thing.

Preempt misfortunes and prepare for them - Stoics are not pessimistic. They are practical people. Regardless of the difficulty involved in a task, they choose to stay and fight. However, they don't fight blindly or in any foolhardy way. They choose to preempt misfortunes and challenges that are likely to hit them and prepare themselves to tackle potential problems. It's like vaccinating yourself against diseases so that you are ready for battle when the time comes.

Called negative visualization by William Irvine, one of the pioneers of the revival of Stoicism in modern times, this attitude is all about arming yourself. Forewarned is forearmed could well be a Stoic-based cliché. The trick is keeping the imagined potential problems as indifferent elements because regardless of the challenges you are going ahead with your plan. Preempting challenges gives you an opportunity to create backup plans.

Seneca said that a wise man encounters little or nothing that he has not expected. We would call a person who wants to face difficulties in life as crazy, right? In the same way, a person who wants a life without any difficulty is also crazy. Therefore, challenges will come, and Stoicism tells you to prepare for them and face them bravely.

Know and accept that outcomes are beyond your control - Taking action, responding after thinking objectively, and keeping a check on your behaviors are all under your control. However, if you do something focusing on all these elements, and still, the results are not as per expectations, know that outcomes are also beyond your control.

You can only do what you can control, and outcomes are outside the purview of your accountability. This attitude helps you manage good and bad outcomes with equanimity. You will find yourself becoming increasingly resilient to failures and 'indifferent' to successes because you will slowly but surely realize that only your actions are under your control, and even the outcomes of those actions are not yours!

Embrace everything in your life - Epictetus said, 'Don't run after the things you love. Instead, love the things that come and happen to you.' Listening to this sound advice will ensure your life is smooth and happy. For example, suppose something you wished for did not happen. What is easy to change? What has happened or your own opinion about the event? The latter, obviously, because that is what is under your control.

This approach is the first step to building a positive attitude in life. How can you change your opinion to make a seemingly undesirable event in your life look good? All you need to do is look for the positive aspects of that event, and your perspective is bound to change too.

Convert all challenges into opportunities - Perception is the key element for this to happen. Look at any obstacle, imaginary or real, and see how you can use it as an opportunity. For example, if you have lost your job, then it is an opportunity to upskill yourself or do the thing you have been putting off because of lack of time and energy. See, you embrace and love everything happening in your life because you choose to look at challenges as opportunities.

Build mindfulness - Remember the commonalities between Stoicism and Buddhism? Well, mindfulness is another common element between these two ways of life. Being mindful of every little action you take and thought you empowers you with profound enlightenment on the ways of the world. You build self-awareness, which, in turn, helps you change your behavior for increasingly positive outcomes.

How to build mindfulness? A simple example is like this. The next time you experience a powerful emotion, step outside, and engage fully with the emotion.

1. What are you feeling?
2. Can you label the emotion?
3. What triggered the feeling?
4. What are the physical sensations?
5. What are the other thoughts running in your head?

When you focus on answering these questions, you'll find yourself becoming detached from the emotion, and you are able to view it objectively. It does not mean you are not feeling the emotion. In fact, mindfulness includes feeling the emotion and pain and joy that come with it.

Mindfulness is about being acutely aware of everything that is happening to you in that particular instant. Mindfulness empowers you to alter your behavior rationally and for the good of everyone concerned including, and especially, yourself.

Therefore, Stoicism was developed and designed to teach its followers how to lead a good life based on love, compassion, and concern for others. This attitude includes not only close family and friends but extends to the world at large so that everyone and everything in this universe can live a fulfilling, meaningful life. The overall welfare of the entire humankind was the basis for the founding of Stoicism, and it's rational, logical, and ethical beliefs.

Impact of Stoicism in the Modern World

In the 1970s, Stoicism started on its revival path regaining the ancient popularity and value as multiple Stoic principles began to be used in Cognitive Behavioral Therapy (or CBT) and logotherapy.

Moreover, authors like Ryan Holiday and William Irvine wrote many books on Stoicism and spread the power of this philosophical thought across the world.

Additionally, modern Stoicism finds a lot of similarities with modern approaches of other ancient schools of philosophy like Buddhism, humanism, determinism, etc.

The crucial question is, 'Is Stoicism relevant today?' The answer is a resounding 'Yes!' Stoicism imparts life skills and life lessons without directly referring to the event or experience. Stoicism teaches you how to manage and overcome life struggles like failures, despair over the loss of a loved one, etc. It teaches you how to handle crippling negative emotions, such as anger, sadness, resentment, jealousy, greed, etc.

Modern life empowers us to work hard and become rich, successful, and famous. However, it does little or nothing to tell us how to deal with grassroots problems of life. For example, look at the older generation in your life. Quite likely, most of them have earned a lot of money and have big, beautiful houses hosting regular, lavish parties. However, if you look closely, few of them are actually happy.

Most of us are so caught up trying to lead a successful life that we have forgotten to lead a happy life. We have lost touch with humanity, which makes us live against what nature ordained for us. As we progress in life, we need to focus on things that make us happy, not rich or famous. And for this, we must build a strong character for which Stoicism is the perfect platform.

Stoicism teaches you to become a practicing philosopher, unlike the many people who go around preaching philosophy and practicing nothing in their daily lives. Philosophy translates into 'lover of wisdom.' Therefore, when you learn a practical school of philosophy like Stoicism, you tend to pick one good habit each day, making you wiser than the previous day. Or at least, you feel compelled to practice the good habit learned so that you are on your way to becoming a wiser person than before. Stoicism helps you do just that.

Practice the four virtues, discard the four vices, and look at everything else with an embracing but ready-to-let-go attitude so that you find more meaning and fulfillment in your life than before. The four cardinal virtues will be your master right through your life.

Chapter 2
STOIC PHILOSOPHERS 101

Historians and philosophers divide the history of Stoicism into three main phases, namely:

1. The Early Stoa
2. The Middle Stoa
3. The Later Stoa.

We have touched on these phases lightly in Chapter 1. Let us look at them in a bit more detail here along with the main philosophers who contributed to each phase.

The Early Stoa

Typically, the early Stoa consists of the period from the founding of Stoicism until Antipater. Some of the most influential Stoics from this period include:

Zeno of Citium (332-262 BC)

As you already by now, Zeno of Citium was the founder of Stoicism and the Stoic Academy (Stoa) in Athens. His life story and the discovery of Stoicism is almost legendary. Before taking the plunge into philosophy, Zeno was a merchant. Once while on a voyage between Phoenicia and Peiraeus, his ship sank and he lost all his cargo and valuables.

He finally ended up in Athens after this disaster. While browsing through a bookstore, Zeno was introduced to and learned about Socrates' philosophy. He was also drawn to the teachings of Crates, another Athenian philosopher. The reading, understanding, and mastery of these philosophical thoughts dramatically altered Zeno's life, and he felt compelled to create, design, and spread another way of life which came to be known as Stoicism.

Zeno is believed to have said to Diogenes Laertius, an ancient Greek philosopher, 'Now that I have lost my everything, including my money and cargo, I am on a good journey.' He is believed to have thanked fate and destiny for the shipwreck because that 'accident' is what drove him towards philosophy.

Zeno started teaching on Stoa Poikile, the Painted Porch, at the marketplace of Agora in ancient Athens. The Stoa Poikile gave rise to Stoicism. Although, multiple additions and changes have taken place in Stoicism since the early teachings of the founder, Zeno, the core value has not changed which is, 'Happiness is nothing but leading a good, flourishing life of fulfillment.' And this good, flourishing life can be had by finding and experiencing peace of mind by living in accordance with nature. After his death, the Athenians honored him and his memory with a bronze statue and a tomb in the Ceramicus at the public cost.

Unfortunately, none of Zeno's works survive, and the only account of him is found in the book, '*Lives and Opinions of Eminent Philosophers,*' written by Diogenes Laertius who was a biographer of Greek philosophers. However, we know that Zeno wrote *Republic*, a book that extols the virtues of having an egalitarian society, an idea in stark contrast to that of Plato. Yes, Plato wrote a book with the same name, which is more popular that Zeno's *Republic*.

Zeno's work does not survive, but Plutarch wrote this about the book, 'No city or town should live with laws that are distinct from each other. We should treat all citizens equally like a flock in which all sheep have access to the benefits of the same pasture.'

Aristo of Chios (c. 260 BC)

Aristo of Chios was a pupil of Zeno, and he is known to have lived and flourished around 260 B.C. His name is often spelled as Ariston too. He was a direct disciple of Zeno. However, he combined the Stoic teachings of Zeno with that of Cynicism to create his own set of beliefs and principles.

He was a strong supporter of the power and importance of learning and mastering ethics. Further, he believed that there is only one virtue to master in this universe, and that is a healthy, intelligent state of mind. Everything else, Aristo said, falls into place. Further,

Aristo believed that being virtuous is sufficient for being happy and fulfilled in life.

He had strong beliefs that only virtue was good, and only vice was bad, and everything else between these two can be treated equally indifferently. His contemporary was Chrysippus who was able to transform Zeno's thoughts into a powerful Stoic narrative resulting in the marginalization of Aristo. Like Zeno, information about Aristo is available to us only through the biographical work of Diogenes Laertius.

Herillus of Carthage (c. 3rd century BC)

Herillus of Carthage was also a pupil of Zeno who lived around 3 B.C. Contrary to most Stoics, Herillus argued that knowledge was the most important aspect, and the true goal of life should be to acquire knowledge rather than to follow virtue. He also divided the pursuit of happiness and fulfillment through two parallel, unconnected paths.

Herillus believed that only scholars and wise men could attain scientific and scholarly knowledge. The second 'lesser goal' of leading a fulfilling life, including performing one's familial and social duties can be achieved by even those who are not wise.

His contemporary Stoics argued contrarily and said that virtue or moral wisdom is the only goal. This moral wisdom lies in working towards and committing oneself to the welfare of other people in society and the world at large. Therefore, Herillus was seen as being skewed towards Aristotelian or Academicians' perspective and was also considered as the extreme opposite of Aristo's stand.

Cleanthes of Assos (330–232 BC)

Cleanthes of Assos was the second head of Stoic Academy (he held this position for 32 years), and he is featured in Diogenes Laertius' biographical work on Greek philosophers. He was born in 331–330 B.C. in Asia Minor and came to Athens in around 281–280 B.C. He held the position of the head of the Stoic

Academy from the time he took over the job from Zeno until his death in 230–229 B.C.

Born in Assos, Cleanthes was a boxer who came to Athens with just four drachmae in his pocket to study philosophy. When he came to Athens to study philosophy, he did not have enough funds. To support his education, Cleanthes of Assos was a water carrier at night. In fact, he was summoned by the court, as no one thought it possible to work so hard and do tough philosophical lessons during the day.

However, the court was so impressed with his intensity for hard work and commitment that they let him go and even offered to pay for his studies. However, Zeno told him not to take charity. As per Diogenes Laërtius, Cleanthes used to attend Crates the Cynic's classes before being introduced to Zeno's philosophy.

Cleanthes' biggest opponent was Aristo of Chios. Cleanthes argued strongly in favor of the importance of physics and logic as much as ethics compared to Aristo, who held that ethics is the only important aspect of Stoicism. In fact, it is the insistence of Cleanthes that

Stoicism today holds physics, logic, and ethics with equal importance, even if ethics has a slightly higher place in the philosophical hierarchy of Stoicism. Cleanthes also defended Zenos' Stoicism against Skepticism.

Cleanthes was an excellent author and is known for four books containing his interpretation of Heraclitus' works and beliefs. Heraclitus' idea was aligned with Zeno's way of natural philosophy. Additionally, Cleanthes authored interpretative works on ancient myth and poetry that supported Zeno's thoughts and ideas.

Parts of his philosophical poetry still survive and include a few lines from 'Hymn to Zeus' and a few lines of the topic of destiny/fate. He is also known to have written about physics, the concept of God, and cosmology. His works are referred to in many of the surviving works of the ancient Greek philosophers.

Chrysippus (c. 280–204 BC)

Chrysippus was the third head of the Stoic Academy who took over from Cleanthes of Assos. Chrysippus was one of the most influential philosophers among the ancient Greeks. He is believed to have had the most influence on Stoicism in those days. He is known for the creation of an empiricist epistemology and psychology that catapulted Stoicism to one of the most popular schools of philosophy until the 2nd century A.D. He proposed multiple Stoic-based alternatives to Aristotle's and Plato's metaphysical theories. He also did a commendable amount of work on Stoic logic, and his system is in sync with modern-day propositional logic.

Chrysippus was born in Soli, which is today known as Mersin, in Turkey. He is believed to have died at the age of 73. He was a pupil of Cleanthes, and, after studying under his master, is known to have become a long-distance/marathon runner. He took over the reins of the Stoic Academy in 230 B.C. after the death of his former master, Cleanthes. The Academy flourished under Chrysippus, and the work done by these early Stoics continued to spread during the Middle Stoa too.

Chrysippus is known to have been a prolific writer, authoring more than 700 books. However, no work of his remains except a few fragments and references in others' books and biographies. Cicero was a contemporary Academic who was also sympathetic to the Stoic cause. It is thanks to Cicero's works that modern historians have been able to put together some semblance to the historical order of Stoicism and Stoic philosophers.

Diogenes of Babylon (230-150 BC)

Diogenes of Babylon is primarily known as the Stoic philosopher who visited Rome in 156-155 B.C., and this visit kindled the interest for Stoicism in the Roman Empire. Born in 230 B.C. in Seleucia in Mesopotamia, Diogenes of Babylon was a student of Chrysippus, the person credited with structuring and systemizing the Stoic philosophy founded by Zeno. Panaetius, the Stoic who popularized Stoicism in Rome, was a disciple of Diogenes.

Antipater of Tarsus (210–129 BC)

Antipater of Tarsus was a successor to Diogenes, and the teacher of Panaetius, the Stoic responsible for the growth and expansion of Stoicism during the Middle Stoa. He was known for his works on divination and gods. Ancient authors like Plutarch speak highly of Antipater and put him along with Zeno, Chrysippus, and Cleanthes. Cicero mentions him as a person with a sharp mind and known to take the lead when it came to debates between his school and the Academy.

Interestingly, he himself had little confidence in his public speaking capabilities and used writing to articulate his thoughts and ideas. Antipater believed God to be incorruptible, blessed being who was concerned about the welfare of humanity. He criticized people who called gods as corrupt and selfish.

The Middle Stoa

The top two Stoic philosophers who lived and spread the word of Stoicism during the Middle Stoa are

Panaetius of Rhodes and Posidonius of Apameia. Let us look at their lives in a bit of detail.

Panaetius of Rhodes (185–109 BC)

Panaetius studied under Diogenes of Babylon as well as Antipater of Tarsus. Panaetius is believed to have spent a lot of time in Rome, especially in the company of P. Cornelius Scipio Aemilianu, an important general and politician of Rome during that time. Panaetius' works and writings have not survived. However, his importance in the spread of Stoicism has survived.

Some sources give us an idea of the thoughts and ideas of Panaetius as he tried to make his mark in the philosophical circle. Here are some ideas that he had disagreements about certain core principles of Stoicism:

- ❖ Panaetius did not believe in divination and the power of the gods.
- ❖ He did not agree to the idea that the universe starts and ends in the primordial fire. He proposed that the universe was everlasting.

- ❖ He also maintained that virtue was not enough to achieve eudaimonia. Some amount of wealth, health, and strength were needed to live a happy, meaningful, and fulfilling life.
- ❖ He also divided virtues into two classes; the contemplative and the practical.

The above ideas, especially the last one, made his contemporary Stoics who believed in and followed the conventional form of Stoicism uneasy and uncomfortable. Also, these ideas of Panaetius illustrated that he wanted to add more Aristotelian and Platonic concepts into Stoicism. Multiple resources from the ancient times attest this desire of Panaetius.

Cicero works also referenced Panaetius, calling him a highly learned scholar. In fact, Cicero's first two books 'On Duties' are based on ideas and thoughts borrowed from Panaetius' On Duty. Three points discussed by Cicero are specifically connected to Panaetius' ideas.

A person who wants to donate or give in charity must choose his beneficiaries sensibly and prudently. You must help those people more who are in closer natural relationship to you than those who are not in close relationship to you. Based on this concept, Cicero (using Panaetius' ideas) develops a natural relationship hierarchy. The closest relationship is through marriage, and the remotest one is through a shared sense of humanity. Everything else fits in between these two extremes.

The next point of Cicero has to do with temperance. Once you have identified the conventional Stoic form of temperance, you must also include your role driven by your natural talents in the display of this virtue in addition to the common, shared humanity connection. Like Panaetius, Cicero argues that temperance should be displayed in accordance with a given circumstance or situation.

The third point of importance given to Panaetius is the spread of Stoicism outside the Hellenic walls. Interestingly, his student Posidonius of Apameia attracted new pupils to Rhodes, and not to Athens for advanced study in Stoicism. With Panaetius' efforts, Stoicism was taught and practiced all across the Mediterranean and was not confined to Athens.

Posidonius of Apameia (c. 135 BC – 51 BC)

Posidonius of Apameia was Panaetius' disciple who was as willing as his master to incorporate Aristotelian and Platonic ideas into Stoicism. Together with Panaetius, Posidonius infused a fresh of breath air into Stoic philosophy, and both are credited with popularizing and epitomizing Stoic principles during the Middle Stoa.

The Middle Stoa philosophy stands at the cusp of early Greek Stoicism and later Roman Stoicism. However, most historians believe that this period did not have much by way of uniqueness because three ancient Greek Stoics and their ideas were still flourishing. Yet, this period stands out because of the ideas of Panaetius and Posidonius that were distinctly different from the other Stoic philosophers during that time.

In fact, the two people's efforts at syncretizing great ideas to produce an even better outcome started a trend of such syncretic efforts as typified by Antiochus of Ascalon in the 1st century A.D.

Hecato of Rhodes (c, 100 BC)

The reason why Hecato of Rhodes comes in this list of prominent Stoic philosophers is the fact his name keeps coming up in many of Seneca's works. Also, he was a disciple of Panaetius. The largest number of quotations in Seneca's works are from Hecato of Rhodes. Here are a few examples:

- ❖ Stop hoping, and you will lose your fears.
- ❖ Be your own friend.
- ❖ If you want to be loved, then you must first love.

Hecato was a prolific writer though none of his works survive today. Diogenes Laërtius mentions six treatises with the authorship of Hecato. These include *On Goods*, *On Virtues*, *On Passions*, *On Ends*, and *On Paradoxes*.

The Later Stoa

Let us look at some of the Stoic philosophers in the Later Stoa period.

Cato the Younger (94–46 BC)

Cato the Younger is known for his intense Stoic life. He lived Stoic principles unfailingly day in and day out. In fact, his actions speak louder than words because he lived the Stoic principle and was not known as much of a writer. During his time, he was a Senator, soldier, an aristocrat, and a hardcore practitioner of Stoic principles.

He was from an aristocratic family (the last in line) that took upon itself to safeguard the ancient and traditional defenders of Roman constitution and culture. His family was one that believed in the duty of protecting the Roman Empire, which grew from nothing to become one of the most powerful and influential governments in those days.

Cato was Julius Caesar's contemporary as well as his archenemy. Cato was a formidable enemy and was considered a great match to Caesar's eloquence, conviction, and personality. Cato the Younger was known for his dawn-to-dusk speech in front of the powerful Roman Senate and also for a 30-day trek he did on foot in the deserts of North Africa.

When the Roman Empire fell, Cato was the last man standing. Cato is an inspiration to multiple modern-day leaders and revolutionary thinkers like George Washington, Benjamin Franklin, John and Abigail Adams, and others.

Seneca the Younger (4 BC – AD 65)

Born in Spain and educated in Rome, Seneca the Younger is one of the most prominent Stoics of all time. His father was Seneca the Elder, a well-known writer in ancient Rome. Seneca the Younger was also the uncle of the famous Roman poet Lucan. Seneca the Younger followed a career in politics and rose to a high-level financial clerk.

His happy life took a bad turn in 41 A.D. when Claudius became the Roman Emperor. Seneca the Younger was exiled to the island of Corsica for allegedly committing adultery with the emperor's niece. From his exile, Seneca wrote a consoling letter to his distraught mother.

But, eight years later, things took a great turn in Seneca's life when Agrippina, Claudius' wife and mother of Nero (the future emperor of Rome) sought permission for his return from Corsica as an adviser and tutor to Nero. Interestingly, Seneca was put to death in 65 A.D. under orders from Emperor Nero, who turned out to be one of the most tyrannical rulers of all time.

The lesson for us about Seneca is this; Stoicism was a constant companion to Seneca right through various stages of his life. Seneca was introduced to Stoicism by Attalus, a Stoic philosopher who was a teacher to young Seneca. Seneca was also highly influenced by Cato whose works and writings were referred often in his own work.

Seneca's most famous Stoicism work is *Letters from a Stoic,* which is recommended even today for people undergoing stress and grief. Also, this book is an insightful resource for people looking for advice on wealth, religion, and power. Here are some of his nuggets of advice:

- ❖ You can soften harsh conditions, open up restricted pathways, lighten up heavy loads in your life, and think your way out of difficult situations.
- ❖ Human beings are not given a short life; we make it short.
- ❖ Human beings have no dearth of supplies; we waste resources given to us.

Gaius Musonius Rufus (1st century AD)

Gaius Musonius Rufus was the mentor for one of the most important Stoic personalities, namely Epictetus. Born in 30 A.D. in Volsinii, Etruria, Musonius became a prominent and revered Stoic teacher until Emperor Nero after uncovering a conspiracy to dethrone him exiled Rufus to a remote island called Gyaros. He returned to Rome at the age of 68 only to be exiled again at the age of 75.

Musonius' idea of philosophy was connected to practical life and answers to questions on how to lead one's life happily and with fulfillment. He focused on the practical aspects of philosophy and did not worry excessively about the theoretical aspects. The only aspect of philosophy that mattered to Musonius was evil and virtue. He argued that human beings could rise above matters of life and death and pain and pleasure and live a contented and meaningful life.

Further, Musonius believed that although we are naturally created to lead a virtuous life, most of us are incapable of doing so until we learn the skills of practical philosophy including discerning between vice and virtue and learning how to live virtuously. Musonius was a highly learned scholar and diligent practitioner of Stoicism. In fact, he is referred to as the Roman Socrates.

Publius Clodius Thrasea Paetus (1st century AD)

Publius Paetus was a Stoic philosopher and Roman senator who lived during the reign of Emperor Nero. Initially, he was treated well by Emperor Nero. However, soon, Publius Paetus realized the tyrannical nature of Nero and openly stood against his dictatorial behavior and attitude.

He argued in front of the Roman Senate for a person who wrote a libel against Emperor Nero to reduce his death sentence to a milder one. This angered Emperor Nero after which the senator was not barred from entering the Senate house. After this incident, it is believed that Publius Paetus lived a private life of simplicity and virtuousness as prescribed by Stoicism.

Epictetus (AD 55–135)

A unique aspect of Stoicism is the fact that people from all walks of life and social hierarchical rank learned and practiced it. For example, Marcus Aurelius was an all-powerful Roman Emperor, Seneca the Younger was a prominent and wealthy Roman citizen who was an adviser to the emperor during his time, and there was Epictetus, a slave, which is, perhaps, the lowest rank in the social hierarchical order of that time. And therein lies the power of the Stoicism. It offers succor for all during good and bad times regardless of class, race, and today, even gender.

Epictetus was born in 55 A.D. Hierapolis, present-day Pamukkale, in Turkey. He was born into a slave family belonging to a wealthy Roman owner named Epaphroditus, who allowed Epictetus to gain an education, which led him to the study of philosophy. Gaius Musonius Rufus was his mentor and teacher.

Epictetus was freed from slavery after the death of Emperor Nero. He then became a Stoic teacher imparting knowledge for over 25 years until Emperor Domitian banished all philosophers from his empire. Epictetus was forced to flee from Rome. He went to Nicopolis in Greece, where he established a philosophy school.

Marcus Aurelius was highly influenced by Epictetus and his teachings. Even today, his teachings and lessons are highly revered by men and women around the world. Interestingly, Epictetus himself did not write anything down. It was his student, Arrian, who wrote down all of his lessons, and this work has helped numerous people right through history find solace, strength, and guidance through their trials and tribulations.

Below are some of his most famous and timeless quotes:

- ❖ We must make the best use of our power and take the rest as it happens.
- ❖ Let the ideas of death and exile always be there in our lives to remind us not to be greedy and covet things unnecessarily.

Hierocles (2nd century AD)

Even though very little information is available about Hierocles, he is an important figure in the history of Stoicism because fragments of his work, *Elements of Ethics*, was discovered in 1901. Additionally, Hierocles is spoken about by Stobaeus, another influential Roman citizen.

The modern Stoics know Hierocles for the creation of concentric circles of concern concept encapsulating the principles of Stoicism. The logic of his concentric circles of concern is based on the idea that the degree of concern we have for people is in direct proportion to the closeness of the relationship.

So, our concern for ourselves is more intense than the concern for our close relatives, which, in turn, is more than our concern for people who are not so closely related to us. Using this reason for concern, it is possible, said Hierocles, to extend our concern even to strangers by increasing our proximity to them. And with this, we can include the entire world into our circle and show care, concern, and love for all human beings.

Marcus Aurelius (AD 121-180)

Born nearly 2000 years ago, this Roman Emperor is, perhaps, the most prominent Stoic leader of all times. Although he was born into a noble, prominent family in Rome, he was not expected to become an emperor. As a young man, he is believed to have loved boxing, wrestling, and hunting, and took the training of these three sports very seriously.

Emperor Hadrian was the ruler of Rome at that time. As he was childless, he adopted Antoninus as his successor. Antoninus was also childless, and as per Hadrian's condition, was to adopt Marcus Aurelius as his successor. Marcus ascended the Roman throne in 161 A.D. after the death of Antoninus, and he ruled for nearly two decades.

During his reign, Rome was faced with multiple problems. There was the menace of the barbarian tribes in the north, the Parthian Empire was continually at war with Rome, the deadly plague left numerous Romans dead, and the rise of Christianity was threatening to finish off the centuries-old Roman culture and tradition.

Marcus was an absolute ruler with immense power. He could have done and got anything he wanted to. However, his greatness lies in the fact that despite access to absolute power, Marcus chose to rule with wisdom and virtue, the basic tenets of Stoicism. He was a true Stoic in all respects, and therefore, is considered as the most important practitioner of this school of philosophy even today.

Marcus allowed himself to rule under the guidance of virtue and wisdom, which is what makes him different from numerous other present and past leaders of the world. His diary, *Meditations*, contain the deepest thoughts of one of the most powerful leaders of all times. This diary has entries in which Marcus has admonished himself to behave virtuously and not give in to temptation. This diary opens our eyes to the intense self-discipline and self-control that Marcus practiced, a key element of Stoicism.

One of the most famous and timeless quotes of Marcus goes like this, 'Don't waste time arguing about how a good man should be. Just be one!'

Chapter 3
Epicureanism Vs. Stoicism

Stoicism and Epicureanism were the two primary schools of philosophy that took birth almost simultaneously during the times of the ancient Greeks. Although the tenets and principles of the two schools differed in their fundamental nature, both Epicureanism and Stoicism agreed that the principal aim of philosophy was to transform people into sages.

So, who is a sage? A sage is one who has achieved 'perfection of being' which is beyond the reach of ordinary mortals like us. In the same vein, trying to achieve perfect wisdom is an unrealizable idea as all human beings are imperfect, and therefore, cannot achieve sagehood. However, even if the pinnacle of sagehood cannot be achieved, it is possible to make progress towards a higher state of perfection than before. This progress or advancement towards a better state of perfection is the ultimate goal of both Epicureanism and Stoicism.

Stereotypically, here is how most people look at Stoicism and Epicureanism:

- ❖ Stoics are emotionless and unfeeling brutes who live in denial of happiness and joy.
- ❖ Epicureans are self-indulgent, pleasure-seeking hedonists.

Now that you have read a lot more about Stoicism, you should already be disagreeing with the stereotypical definition of Stoicism, right? The same misconception holds true for Epicureanism as well. Most often, stereotypes fall way too short of the truth to be taken seriously in any way. But, these definitions are a grave injustice to two of the most vibrant and powerful philosophies created and designed by the ancient wise men.

Epicureanism and Stoicism were founded around 300 B.C. in Athens because the lives of the founders, Epicurus and Zeno respectively, overlapped. Both of them advised that excessive desires and pleasure are not a good thing. Just like how Stoics were not advised to become emotionless and unfeeling, the early Epicureans were not taught to self-indulge excessively as the misconception exists today.

Moreover, Stoicism did not hesitate to borrow good and effective philosophical ideas from other schools, including Epicureanism. For example, Seneca the Younger did write a strong critique against some of the tenets of Epicureanism in his book, *Letter from a Stoic*. However, you can find numerous works in which he has praised and quoted some of the tenets and principles of Epicureanism.

A crucial element that differentiates true seekers of wisdom from fundamentalists is that true seekers are fine with embracing all things that make sense and are worthy of learning. On the other hand, fundamentalists get so carried away with their own school of thought that they believe that everything outside of it is unworthy. Seneca the Younger was a true seeker of wisdom, and he was willing to incorporate elements from other schools of thought providing he was convinced of its value.

Let us look deeply into these two systems of philosophies and how they are different and similar too.

What is Epicureanism?

Epicureanism is a philosophy that considers pleasure as the highest good. However, before reading too much into the word 'pleasure' in this context, let us understand more about Epicureanism. Epicurus, the founder of this school of philosophy, realized that human beings are miserable because we desire things that are not needed for happiness and peace of mind.

Therefore, if we could learn and practice the art of desiring only those elements of life that are necessary and natural, then we need not be miserable. Epicurus thought that we could bathe in the simple 'joy of being' by ensuring our basic needs are satisfied. An Epicurean sage is one who can enjoy the sheer pleasure of being by simply getting his basic needs like food, clothing, shelter, etc. met. In fact, such a sage could rival the happiness of the gods!

This school of philosophy believes that nature has designed us in such a way that achieving certain goals and purposes in our life brings us happiness, and therefore, it is natural to seek these goals in life. Epicurus believed that even reason teaches us that pain is bad and pleasure is good, and therefore, seeking pleasure cannot be a bad thing.

However, it is important to balance this seeking attitude as overindulgence leads to pain too. Epicureanism teaches you to avoid this kind of pain too, and to do this, Epicurus divided pleasure into three types, including:

1. Natural and necessary
2. Natural and not necessary
3. Not natural and not necessary

Of these three categories, Epicureans are allowed to seek only the first type, namely the natural and necessary one. These kinds of pleasures are easy to obtain, and they are sufficient for peace of mind, which is the ultimate goal of Epicureanism. Examples of natural and necessary pleasures are having enough to eat and drink, a good home for shelter, and friends and family for social interaction. Most other things of pleasure fall into the second and third category, which brings pain, and therefore, should be avoided.

For example, seeking sexual pleasure, having children, or being popular are natural but not necessary. Therefore, it is better to avoid running after these elements excessively so as to keep your life simple, thereby avoiding suffering.

The third category of pleasure is to be completely avoided, and this core Epicurean belief is sufficient to discard the myth connecting this school of philosophy to hedonism and self-indulgence. Unnatural and unnecessary pleasures like the use of alcohol, seeking excessive sexual pleasures, etc. are to be avoided completely. Epicurus warned his followers that a person who is not satisfied with little would not be satisfied with anything.

Additionally, Epicurus divided pleasure into two different types, including static and moving. 'Moving pleasures' are those that involve the process of satisfying a desire. For example, having a meal to satiate your hunger is a 'moving pleasure.' 'Static pleasures' are those experiences that come from the feeling of having your desires satiated. For example, feeling satiated after a meal is a 'static pleasure.'

According to Epicurus, 'static pleasures' are better as there is no need or want during the experience. Also, Epicureanism differentiates between mental and physical pleasures and pains. This school of philosophy argues that anxieties and uncertainty about the future and fear of death and gods are the biggest obstacles to achieving happiness. It is important to get rid of anxiety and fear to be happy.

Gods and Epicureanism - Epicurus believed that gods existed. However, he said that they did not care for or were even unaware of the existence and problems of humankind. In fact, he believed that the gods did not want to interfere with the lives and problems of humankind because it could lead to the compromise of their own characteristic tranquil and happy nature. Therefore, human beings should try and achieve the supreme happiness and peace of mind that gods enjoy instead of fearing them.

Death and Epicureanism - Epicurus urged his followers not to fear death too. Here are some pointers for this belief:

- ❖ The mind is part of the human body that, like all things in the universe, is made up of atoms.
- ❖ When a person dies, these atoms are disintegrated and re-dispersed, and the person ceases to exist.
- ❖ As the individual does not exist anymore after death, he or she cannot be troubled.
- ❖ If death cannot cause trouble after a person dies, how can it cause harm when the person is alive, argued Epicurus.
- ❖ The eternity existing before the birth of an individual is not considered harmful. In the same way, the eternity existing after the death of the individual cannot be considered harmful.

All these arguments meant that death is an element of human life that should not be feared.

Pleasure and Epicureanism - Like Aristotle, Epicurus believed that happiness is an end by itself and is the highest good of human life. However, unlike Aristotle, Epicurus said that pursuit of pleasure by avoiding pain is what will deliver happiness and not logic, reason, or ethics. He said that pleasure is the highest virtue, and the power of everything else is limited to the temporary pleasure that it can deliver.

He argued that infant behavior, which is based on instinctive pursuit of pleasure, is the best proof that pleasure is the highest good. Human beings can immediately sense pleasure and pain, just like how we can instinctively sense whether something is cold or hot, wet or dry, dull or colorful, etc. All actions of human beings, including the so-called altruistic and virtuous ones, are nothing but pleasure-seeking behaviors.

Of course, Epicurus warned repeatedly that we must not pursue all kinds and degree of pleasure-giving elements. Also, he said that not all kinds of pain should be avoided. We must calculate the highest pleasure that can be obtained from a particular experience, behavior, or attitude, and make prudent sensible choices to achieve as close as a sage-like personality as possible.

Thus, Epicureanism is a philosophy that emphasized the importance of training and moderating one's desires to achieve peace of mind.

Who are the Epicureans?

Epicureanism was not designed as a dry philosophical school relegated only to theoretical knowledge. The tenets of Epicureanism were created to help people live freely and happily without the burdens of baseless anxieties and worries weighing down on them. In this context, Epicureanism is relevant even today, and the modern Epicurean follows and practices the following tenets of Epicureanism:

- ❖ Do not fear God.
- ❖ Do not be scared of death.
- ❖ Do not be afraid of pain.
- ❖ Live and lead a simple life.
- ❖ Pursue happiness through the pursuit of pleasure, prudently and wisely.

- Make as many friends as you can, and you should also be a good friend to others.
- Practice honesty both in your professional and personal life.
- Avoid politics, popularity, and fame.

An Epicurean is one who cherishes and values prudence, self-management, self-sufficiency, serenity, simplicity, friendliness, honesty, generosity, cheerfulness, and gentleness.

Top Quotations of Epicureanism that Have Withstood the Test of Time

Don't spoil the happiness of enjoying what you have by desiring what you don't have. Remember that the things you have now are what you had hoped for earlier.

The art of living and dying well are the same.

Our abundance in life is constituted by what we enjoy and not by what we possess.

If a man does not find satisfaction with little, then he is unlikely to find satisfaction with anything.

It is foolhardy for a man to pray to the gods to get things for which he has the power to get.

It is foolish to try and cater to a crowd because it does not approve of my choices, and I don't know what they approve.

The misfortune of a wise man is always better than the prosperity of a foolish man.

Differences Between Stoicism and Epicureanism

Stoicism teaches that the highest good in the world is to live virtuously and justly. Stoics are taught to treat pain and pleasure indifferently. Epicureans, on the other hand, believe that we should maximize our pleasure by minimizing or eliminating our pain. Epicureanism teaches that pleasure is the beginning and end of a good, happy, and fulfilling life.

For Stoics, virtue was the foundation and guiding principle of their life. For Epicureans, virtue was a means to an end, which is nothing but pleasure.

Epicureanism taught its followers to live simply and by forming strong relationships with other people. Stoicism taught people to fully and wholly embrace the ways of nature.

Epicureans believed that when we die, the atoms of our bodies get disorganized and disintegrated, and we no longer exist. Epicurus said that the terrible thing called death is nothing for us because when we exist, then death doesn't, and when death exists, we don't exist. Therefore, Epicureanism taught that by giving up the fear of death, gods, and divination, we could live without anxiety, which in turn helps us maximize the pleasure of life.

The Stoics believed in the existence of gods and divination, and it is crucial to align our lives virtuously and in accordance with nature. Epictetus, the famous Stoic philosopher, said, 'We are all small appendages of Zeus, the God of Gods, and who are we as appendages to question the plans of nature and God!'

The Stoics and Epicureans also differed drastically on the ways of avoiding pain. The Stoics believe that pain is a result of our own perceptions, and if we can change our outlook, the pain can be eliminated, or at least, minimized. For example, the Stoics believed that we have the power to choose or not choose to suffer if something bad happened to us. So, while pain is inevitable, suffering is a choice each of us makes based on our perceptions.

Epicureans believe that we can avoid pain and suffering by overcoming the fear of death and gods. Also, according to Epicureanism, pain can be avoided by not desiring things that are unnatural and unnecessary. It is possible to find happiness and peace of mind if you live simply and create strong bonds of friendships with people you can trust.

Epicureans believe in the concept of 'living hidden' which means to live away from public life, by avoiding complex desires, and by staying close to your home. The Stoics do not believe in staying away from public life or withdrawing from society in any way. In fact, Stoics believe that all of us have an obligation to society, and public life can exist only when everyone participates in it. A Stoic strongly believes that everyone has a role to play in society, and he or she has to fulfill regardless of how small or humble the role may appear. Failure to participate in society amounts to failing to live up to an important cardinal virtue, namely justice.

Both Stoics and Epicureans believe in not harming other people and also upholding the law without breaking established rules and regulations. However, the reasons for these beliefs are different for Stoics and Epicureans. The Stoics' reason is based on virtue as it is central to their philosophy, and breaking laws and harming others are vices that one should avoid.

The Epicureans' reason was more practical; they believe harming others or breaking the law is likely to make you scared, and consequently, you will be distracted from happiness. Epicureans claim that injustice by itself is not evil. However, the consequences of unjust behavior are bound to lead to reduced happiness and increased fear, which is against the core beliefs of Epicureans. Of course, Epicureans have no answer to the question that people who break laws are the ones who don't feel bad or fear about doing the activity.

Another reason for Epicureans not to harm others is their belief in an unwritten social contract or agreement not to harm each other. Morality in Epicureanism is formulated on this agreement on social contact. Also, building of strong friendships is an important core principle of Epicureanism. Therefore, treating them well is a crucial element in this school of philosophy, as this attitude will make your friends loyal to you.

Friendships in Epicureanism were seen as a 'fair-weather' kind of relationship because it was based on mutual self-interest. This approach is in stark contrast to Stoicism, where friendships are based on common likes and dislikes and with mutual admiration for each other's character and personality.

If you were a Stoic, then in genuine friendships, you would put the interest of your friend above your own. Contrarily, in Epicureanism, virtue is seen only as a means to an end, and consequently, having good friends is a means to achieving happiness and fulfillment.

Although the paths of the Stoics and Epicureans might appear dissimilar, and the ultimate goals are contrary to each other, both Stoicism and Epicureanism taught people how to avoid pain. In Stoicism, pain is avoided by accepting and embracing the ways of nature and whatever is happening to you, even if you don't like it. In Epicureanism, natural and necessary urges are to be accepted and efforts made to satisfy them. In Stoicism, it is acceptable that natural and necessary urges including basic hunger and thirst to go unsatisfied, and it is virtuous to embrace these difficulties too as being part of the ways of nature and/or destiny.

Chapter 4
Psychology & Mindset Mastery

Now that you know Stoicism consists of timeless and practical tenets, it makes sense to spend some time to learn how you can use Stoic principles and ideas to master your mindset and build your psychological strength to lead an improved and better life than before.

Stoics were the pioneers in the discovery of what is today known as 'soft skills.' Soft skills are becoming increasingly important in all fields to help people enhance productivity and build positive and harmonious work environments in their professions regardless of their domain.

Self-Awareness and Stoicism

Our characteristic behaviors and attitudes are excellent clues and give us immense insight into our strengths and weaknesses. This self-awareness is a powerful tool for improving our lives. The concept of self-awareness is an idea that seems to have been borrowed from Socrates. Epictetus loved the following Socrates quote, 'Some people love to improve their farm, and some people revel in improving the performance of their horse. In the same way, I delight in improving myself daily.'

Heraclitus, another ancient Greek philosopher who influenced Stoic thoughts, especially Marcus Aurelius, also emphasized the importance of building self-awareness. Heraclitus said, 'Our conceited opinions and the lack of self-awareness drives us to ignorance and prevent us from seeing the reality in our lives.' Therefore, building self-awareness is one of the most crucial elements of Stoicism.

Stoics understood how easy it is to get into the habit and thought patterns, and not wanting to leave the comfort zone of these habits, we choose to find opinions that justify our irrational behavior. As we become increasingly comfortable in our cocoons, we stop making efforts to become self-aware. Instead, we get ourselves wrapped up in our patterns and habits, and consequently, get further away from our reality than before.

Stoics use the following two concepts to break limiting thought and behavior patterns in our lives that help us increase our self-awareness.

- ❖ Become suspicious of your own behaviors, thoughts, and opinions until you have proven them to be correct.
- ❖ Become sympathetic to other people's behaviors, thoughts, and opinions before being suspicious.

Further, Stoics urge you to take time out and think rationally before you get carried away by your own thoughts and feelings. Epictetus said, 'Tell your opinions and thoughts to hold off for a bit until you have had time to test and reason out their validity and prudence.'

The Stoics continually use Epictetus' concept of 'dokimazo' which translates 'to test and analyze.' Stoicism urges its followers to analyze and test one's thoughts, opinions, and behaviors without judgment so that our self-awareness increases. Most of us form opinions based on prejudices and biases, and consequently, our opinions are colored and not necessarily true. Stoicism teaches you to make observations about everything, including yourself non-judgmentally.

When we practice self-awareness, we can discern between fake thought or feeling or behavior from a genuine one, just like experienced bankers can distinguish between a counterfeit coin and a good one. We can sense and identify our unauthentic thoughts and behaviors just like how musicians can filter out bad musical notes from a harmony.

Interestingly, when you are gauging other people and their behaviors, Stoicism says you must flip the exercise mentioned above. First, show sympathy and compassion, and only after thorough analysis, you are allowed to be suspicious. Marcus Aurelius was one of the most powerful people alive during his time, and he could have done or got what he wanted anytime any day. However, he chose compassionate wisdom over an exhibition of power.

His wise words about gauging other people go something like this, 'Whenever another behavior or attitude offends or irritates you, step back from the emotion and look within yourself. Identify those experiences or events when you have done wrong or misused power given to you. When you turn your thoughts towards your own failings, then the anger you feel for others is bound to dissipate, and you will be able to see why they are behaving the way they do. If you can, then don't hesitate to help such people too.'

Marcus Aurelius' humility and sense of humanity were deeply rooted in Stoic ideas. He observed that all human beings are like trainees trying to do our best. We must remember this humble thought, even when life is seemingly unfair and unreasonable. This great emperor uses the metaphor of wrestling to explain his thought process. He says this:

'When we are fighting in the ring, and we get scratched, hit, and hurt during the fight, we don't complain, do we? You don't view your opponent as being wrong or not following the rules. You simply keep an eye on him so that you can avoid the worst punches. Well, the world is one big fighting ring. Everyone does his or her bit to survive, and in the process, unintentional harming of other people is bound to take place. We must accept it as the way of nature.'

Therefore, Stoicism reiterates two simple strategies to build self-awareness. First, view your behaviors and attitude with suspicious, and second, view others' behaviors and attitude with sympathy.

Many modern psychologists have based their therapies and modern-day 'soft skills' training program on Stoicism and its principles and values. One great example of such Stoicism-inspired psychologists is Travis Bradbury, who developed on Daniel Goleman's work on emotional intelligence, by adding Stoic strategies to increase self-awareness as a tool to improve one's quality of life. In fact, the first step to developing emotional intelligence is by building self-awareness.

Here are some suggestions that can be incorporated into your life too:

Look at your feelings and emotions without judgment. Your emotions are going to be there regardless of whether you like them or don't. Therefore, instead of being overly carried away by their effects, it is wise to experience your emotions and understand them without judgment. You can use the learning from this non-judgmental experience of self-awareness to make behavioral and attitudinal changes for self-improvement.

Observe your emotions like a hawk. Become a third-party observer of your feelings. Just like how a hawk can catch the subtlest of movements that its prey is making even from a great height, you must practice building your ability to catch the slightest change in your emotions. This approach improves self-awareness significantly as you become increasingly sensitive even to subtle changes. Taking a third-party view of your emotions helps immensely to remove all kinds of judgments. You have to literally detach yourself from your emotions, and catch impulsive attitudes like how a sharp-eyed hawk catches its prey.

Observe the physical effects of your emotions. Most of our feelings result in physical effects on our body too. For example, when we feel fear, we feel a tingling in our neck as our hair stands up. Also, we feel a pit-like formation being formed in our stomachs due to fear. Our heart beats faster than normal. Some of us get sweaty palms. Become aware of these changes in your body and focus on them without trying to control them. These non-judgmental observations of physical changes also improve your self-awareness significantly.

Look at the ripple effect of your emotions. When you see your emotions objectively, then instead of engaging with them, you are literally stepping back to see how they affect your behavior and those of others around you. For example, if you consciously reacted to your anger by scolding someone, then the ripple effect of your emotion is the feelings created in the other person. By stepping out of your emotions, you are preventing yourself from impulsive reactions, which empowers you to see the potential and real ripple effects of your feelings.

Become comfortable with negative emotions. Most of us don't like to look at negative emotions, and frequently, brush them under the carpet as if they did not exist. This approach is counterproductive to building self-awareness. You must look at all your emotions, including the not-so-pleasant ones and acknowledge their existence. This is the first step to managing negative emotions because if you don't accept there is a problem, how will you find solutions for it?

The push-and-pull with other people in our lives should not be treated like an obstruction or obstacle. These struggles are happening as per the natural order of things. So, instead of complaining about them, it is wise to embrace them, and accept them into your life. Consequently, you will find that managing stresses and anxieties will not become such as bother as it is today.

In fact, every time we engage with other people (even in the form of conflict), it is a chance to learn more about yourself and others in the conflict or the engagement. When we look at conflicts as opportunities, we are able to become more productive and efficient in our lives.

Seneca the Younger said that it is possible to remove nearly all our sins from our body and mind if we simply learn to look at and become aware of them first. Once you are aware and accept the things that are going wrong in your life, then you can find umpteen solutions to overcome these mistakes.

Stoics Vs. Non-Stoics

A Stoic works like a master archer. What does an archer do? He focuses all his energies to hit the target. However, hitting the target is not an archer's end result. His result is in becoming a better archer each day. His happiness lies in his ability to shoot well, which does not necessarily include hitting the target every time he shoots.

A Stoic understands and appreciates the fact that effort to become a good archer is in his hands. Hitting the target has multiple factors that are beyond his control. So, he chooses to focus only on what he can control and lets go of things that are not under his control. A Stoic thinks in the same way. Stoics focus their energies and resources on what they can control and do not fret and worry about elements that are not in their control.

A Stoic's art of living is in accepting that an outcome is dependent on factors that are way beyond his or her control. Therefore, a Stoic will work on things that he can manage so that the stress of what he cannot manage does not hinder his complete experience with each moment. Stoics believe that the most expert archer in the world cannot control the outcome of hitting the target every time. Therefore, an expert archer is one who only works at improving his skills at all times.

The primary difference between a Stoic and a non-Stoic is that the former is acutely aware of things he or she can control while the latter is so caught up with uncontrollable elements that he or she forgets to do what needs to be done. A non-Stoic person works like an amateur archer while a Stoic works like a master archer.

Taking your focus off elements that you cannot control also helps you eliminate stress. The acceptance of the inevitable takes away the fear of uncertainty. Eugen Herrigel wrote a book titled *Zen in the Art of Archery* in which he describes the experience of learning archery from a Japanese Zen master. The master made the act of shooting look effortless, whereas Eugen was under excessive stress.

One of the most significant challenges for Eugen was to relax during shooting practice. He tried to hit the target multiple times, and each time he failed, his stress increased. And his master was able to hit the target without anxiety and fear. Why? Because the master was focused on building his skill. He was not concerned about whether he will hit his target or not.

The master knew the outcome was outside his zone of control. Eugen, on the other hand, was wasting his efforts on trying to control the uncontrollable outcome instead of working on building his shooting skills. Eugen's master said that if you hit the target every time, then it means you are a trickster trying to show off your skills. Instead, he said, take your mind off the external outcome, and focus on stabilizing yourself internally. When Eugen realized this powerful truth, he was able to let go of stress and anxiety. This attitude is what a Stoic aims to achieve: to focus on what he or she can do and forget about what he or she cannot do.

When Eugen finished his archery course with the Japanese master, he realized that even though he has become a good archer, the bigger change was his internal self. He was a different personality when he graduated from archery school. He underwent internal changes and that is what helped him achieve happiness and peace of mind.

A Stoic's goal is internal to himself or herself. Changes have to be made within for outward changes to happen. A non-Stoic, on the other hand, will look at outward changes to happen to make internal changes, if at all. As the internal remains unchanged, a non-Stoic does not find happiness. As internal changes are happening in the right way, a Stoic will find happiness regardless of the external influences.

Stoics allow themselves to be led by and flow with nature. They immerse themselves in the moment and engage with it fully. Non-Stoics typically (and mostly, unwittingly) contradict their life with the ways of nature, and therefore, find themselves in a constant struggle against the flow.

For the Stoics, the real goal is internal. An external goal is entirely non-existent in the life of a Stoic. Whereas non-Stoics are continually trying to achieve success and fame, Stoics are constantly working on improving themselves regardless of the circumstances of the external world. That is why a Stoic can be happy if he is poor or rich, healthy or unhealthy, with or without resources, with or without friends and family, or in any other state.

How to Develop a Stoic Mindset?

Building a Stoic mindset is not rocket science. The ideas of Stoicism are extremely simple. The trick is in implementing the Stoic concepts unfailingly in your daily life. Let us look at some suggestions, tips, and recommendations to develop a Stoic mindset.

Accept the things you cannot change - World events, natural disasters, political upheavals, and most other things that are happening at a world level are rarely in your hands. In fact, it would be wise to assume that these things are not even entirely in the hands of powerful world leaders. So, why fret over such things that you cannot do anything about? Simply accept them as events that are meant to happen.

Focus on things you can change like your choices, likes, dislikes, etc. Focus on how you build judgments because you are at liberty to alter these opinions because they are directly under your control.

For example, if you don't like someone, it is well within your control to change your feelings towards that person. You can choose to like the person from this moment onwards, and nothing in the world can really make you dislike the concerned individual. The reverse is also true. You could like a not-so-good person blindly, and it takes a moment for you to see the truth and begin disliking him or her.

If you are playing a game, some of the things you cannot control are:

- ❖ Your opponent's strengths and weaknesses.
- ❖ The judgment of the referee.
- ❖ The movement of wind or the coming of rain.

However, you can control how much you practice before the actual match instead of wasting time partying all night. Even if you do not win the game, you would definitely become a better player than before. Therefore, accept what you cannot change and focus on what you can.

Think before you act or speak - Improve your self-awareness by observing your emotions and reactions. Practice self-discipline by giving yourself time before you react impulsively to anything that is happening around you or even to you. Spend some time understanding your thoughts, where they are coming from, what others are saying and why, and other such elements before choosing to act or speak.

For example, if someone has hurled an insult at you, don't counter it with an insult. Instead, step out of the experience, and ask yourself if there is any truth in what has been said to you. If yes, you could use it as feedback for self-improvement. If it is no, there is absolutely no need to act or respond. You could simply walk away and let the insult boomerang on the speaker.

Use visualization techniques if you find it difficult to be objective in an unpleasant environment. For example, if you have not been able to step away from the unpleasant situation where someone insulted you, then close your eyes, and imagine a pleasant picture in your mind. It could be your favorite spot like the beach or a mountain top from where you see the beauty of nature unfold before you. This positive visualization is a powerful tool to help you manage negative situations.

Alternately, you can use Stoic affirmations (see more ideas below) like, 'If this is not under my control, then it is not my concern.' All these simple and effective tools help you ground yourself while giving you time to control your emotions so that you can act or speak more responsibly and maturely than before.

Don't build your life based on other people's reactions - Stop worrying about what other people think of you and your life. You are not obliged to conform to anyone's expectations and living standards. If you are not as rich as your friend, so be it. A Stoic does not need riches to be happy.

Don't get nervous when talking to people who seem to come from higher strata of society because remember that these elements are to be treated indifferently by Stoics. These things are not required for happiness and peace of mind. Live your life on your terms without causing harm to others around you. Don't feel the burden of the obligation of behaving in a certain way only to please people. Develop your own set of morals and build your life around them.

In the modern language, a good way of putting this point is by telling you not to outsource your happiness because no one else but you are responsible for and capable of bringing this crucial Stoic component into your life.

Be humble and always be a learner - No human being knows everything there is to know in this universe. We are all students trying to learn as much as we can. Therefore, always be humble and be ready to learn at every given opportunity. Building knowledge and wisdom is a core Stoic virtue, and you can cultivate wisdom only when you are in a humble, learning mode. One thing that the modern world does not lack is the availability of learning resources. Here are some of them:

- ❖ Read as many books as you can.
- ❖ Listen to podcasts if you don't enjoy reading.
- ❖ Watch documentaries and informative videos like TEDTalks etc. to learn more about technology, nature, art, the working of the human mind, and numerous other topics that interest you.
- ❖ William Irvine's books of Stoicism can be a great start to delve into this fascinating school of philosophy.

The trick is to build an attitude of learning that never wanes in strength. Always be a student, and you are likely to achieve Stoic-inspired wisdom sooner than later.

Develop a fair-minded attitude - Stoicism avoids all kinds of retributions, revenge, conflicts, and everything that comes in the way of being humble, kind, and compassionate. Of course, this does not mean you should be cold and unemotional. It only means that if someone chooses to hurt or wrong you, then instead of countering them with a similar harsh attitude, you can choose to be sympathetic towards them.

After all, it is not your problem that they behave badly and insultingly. Moreover, wasting your energy and time in needless emotional conflicts leaves you feeling tired and unprepared to handle the important aspects of your life.

For example, if someone chooses to say something nasty to you, you don't have to walk away. You could walk up to the person, and say, 'I think it is unfair you are behaving this way. Let us cool down and talk things over respectfully and civilly.' Also, taking revenge is completely non-Stoical in approach. So, avoid trying to get even with people who have hurt you. Instead, forgive them, and get on with your life.

Stoic Exercises and Practices for Everyday Life

Leading a happy, productive life is a key element of Stoicism. Here are some tips for the same:

Avoid Distractions - The most precious commodity in this world is time, and Stoics have always believed that we should be tight-fisted about time rather than about money and property. Therefore, you must not waste it on distractions that prevent you from achieving what you want to achieve. This suggestion is one of the most difficult in today's distraction-filled world, considering multiple elements vie for your attention.

Even if you were to lock yourself in a room to work on a project or assignment, umpteen other technology-based elements try and distract you from work. Notifications from emails, social media platforms, news feeds, etc. are highly time-consuming and wasteful activities that deter you from your life purpose. Be wary of all distractions and take steps to eliminate or at least minimize their effect.

Practice the art of remaining focused on your current job or task even if you are bothered by distractions.

Live and engage in the moment - Every moment of your life is precious, beautiful, and meaningful. You don't have to be an antisocial or emotionless person to live each moment meaningfully. You just need to make your entire being live in the moment. For example, if you are having a coffee break, sip your coffee, and revel in its taste, texture, flavor, smell, etc. If you are doing an assignment, make sure you are entirely immersed in the work, and your body and mind are fully engaged with that particular assignment.

A Stoic will look at a glass of wine he is drinking and contemplate, 'What if this were the last glass of wine I get to drink?' If such a situation were to happen, wouldn't you make sure that you enjoy every little sip of that wine? Think of every moment in the same way, and know and appreciate that the present moment is the only moment under your control.

Don't stress yourself about the small stuff in your life - You have spilled milk, paid a couple of dollars more than necessary for the parking, or don't have the perfect dress for the party, etc. These are little annoyances that will keep coming up in your life.

Don't fret excessively about this little stuff because then you will not have the time and energy for the big stuff in your life like following your passion, doing well in school, getting a good job, etc. Remember to recognize the small stumbles and pains in your life, smile, and carry on with your work.

Surround yourself with positive people - Stoics do not isolate themselves from society. They are active participants because they believe that we have a social and familial duty to fulfill. However, remember you are the average of the five people you keep the company of. Therefore, try and surround yourself with like-minded, positive people so that you can also build the same mindset.

Spend time with people who want to become wiser and happier than before. Surround yourself with people whom you respect for the way they lead their lives. Keep the company of compassionate and kind people so that some of their attitudes can rub off on you.

Have friends who encourage you to learn and gain more knowledge. Avoid friends who spend time wasting on distractions and other happiness-denting aspects of life.

Keep out negative, vindictive, judgmental, and petty people from your life.

Value virtue and morals more than material gains - Of course, we want material gains like money and wealth because they can contribute to our happiness. However, material elements cannot solely contribute to our happiness. We must be happy internally for external joy to affect our lives positively.

For example, if you have gained money by cheating people, you are unlikely to be happy even if the society views you as a successful person. Then, the softest and the most luxurious of beds cannot give you peaceful sleep at night because your inner self is gnawing at your soul. Therefore, value virtue and morals over material gains. Like the Epicureans, try and find happiness in simple things of life.

Additionally, throw out ego, vanity, and pride out of the window. These are the biggest obstacles to achieving a Stoic-inspired happy, contented, and purposeful life. And finally, a true Stoic knows that nothing in this world endures. The entire universe is temporary and will cyclically move in and out of the primordial fire.

Building Mindfulness with Stoic Affirmations and Meditations

Use the following meditation- and affirmation-based techniques to help build mindfulness, one of the most crucial aspects of Stoicism. So, what is mindfulness? It is the awareness arising from being fully present in the moment and engaging with everything happening within and around you. Mindfulness techniques help in building self-awareness, a key element of Stoicism. So, let us get to its discussion right away.

Visualize your place in this world - Recall Hierocles' concept of Concentric Circles, and use it as a tool to identify your place in this world. Follow these steps:

- ❖ Visualize yourself and think of your personality, strengths, and weaknesses. You will be in the innermost circle.
- ❖ Next, visualize your friends and family in a circle around you. Who are your friends and

family? Who fits into the circle closest to you? Put all these people in that close first circle around you.

- ❖ Then, put your acquaintances, not-so-close friends and family members, neighbors, and other people into another circle, which is further away from you than the first one.
- ❖ Put your city and state in the next circle.
- ❖ Put your country in the next circle.
- ❖ Put the world in the next circle.
- ❖ Put the universe that you can imagine in the next circle.

It might take about 10-15 minutes to complete this exercise. Sit quietly in an undisturbed place, and focus on these concentric circles. This exercise helps you understand where and why you fit into the grand scheme of things divined by the gods and the powers that are beyond human beings. Also, this visualization helps you understand how everything in this world is interconnected.

Visualize a big loss or something really bad - This is a powerful Stoic-based meditation technique in which you visualize losing something that is very dear to you. It could be your job that provides for your family or even the death of a loved one. Just for a few seconds, picture this negative experience. Yes, it is bound to be a disturbing feeling. But, the point of this seemingly cruel exercise is to remind you about the impermanence of nature and how life will go on regardless of what happens to you or your loved ones.

Also, visualizing a negative event helps you prepare for the worst scenario while reiterating the need for being grateful for the multiple good things in your life. Aren't we great at taking things for granted? This exercise helps you remain grounded and builds awareness that anything can happen anytime. Yet, we must learn to live and enjoy every moment.

Negative visualization also helps to build resilience to overcome obstacles and challenges of life. You might find it easier to handle difficult real-life situations if you have enough practice through negative visualizations.

Read one great Stoic quote daily and reflect on it - Every day, identify one quote from a Stoic philosopher and reflect on its meaning. Also, keep repeating the quote throughout the day even as you try and contemplate on it. Think of how quotes written more than 2000 years ago are still relevant and wonder about the magical aspect of human beings. Remind yourself that no matter how advanced our technology becomes, deep down we human beings are the same as our ancestors were when it comes to pondering life and its mysteries. Here are some quotes to get you started. You are likely to find a lot more as you keep reading books and listening to podcasts on Stoicism.

- ❖ Do not waste time arguing what a good man should do; just do it - Marcus Aurelius.
- ❖ Don't procrastinate your actions, don't confuse your conversations, and don't wander and get lost in your thoughts. - Marcus Aurelius.
- ❖ The best revenge is to not be like your opponent or enemy - Marcus Aurelius.
- ❖ We are more often frightened than hurt. We suffer a lot more in our imaginations than in our reality - Seneca

- If a man does not know which port he wants to land in, then no wind can be favorable for him. - Seneca
- Nothing is a better proof of a well-ordered man than to stop where he is right now and spend a little time in his own company. - Seneca
- A man who fears death will do anything worthy when he is alive. - Seneca
- First, tell yourself what you want to be, and then do what you have to do. - Epictetus
- Don't explain your philosophy of life. Live and embody it. - Epictetus

Start and maintain a reflective journal - Journaling is a powerful tool for self-awareness and self-improvement. At the end of each day, spend a few minutes writing down the highlights of the day. Find answers to the following questions and write them down in your journal:

- What are the challenges you faced?
- What are the decisions you took?
- Did you do anything to eliminate a bad habit?

- ❖ If given another chance, would you do things differently? What is the progress you would have made?

Journaling is an act of forced self-reflection that compels us to face both pleasant and unpleasant experiences objectively and with equanimity. It is a powerful tool for mindfulness. The benefits of journaling are many including:

- ❖ Boosts creativity
- ❖ Improves our sense of gratitude
- ❖ Serves as a form of self-therapy

When you write your feelings and thoughts down, they become clearer than when they were in your mind. The ancient Stoics were keenly aware of the power of journaling. Marcus Aurelius, one of the most powerful men in his time, would diligently write in his diary every day, observing his thoughts, feelings, and experiences. This diary is what we know today as Marcus Aurelius' *Meditations*, a book that nearly Stoics have read and been benefited. Yet, there is little doubt that the biggest benefactor of these journals was Marcus himself. The sense of accountability and clarity of thought that his diary gave him helped him make the right choices in life. The effects of these choices have lasted over 2000 years as even modern Stoics are learning and gaining wisdom from his journal.

Being a Stoic is not difficult. It only requires diligent and persistent efforts until the thinking process becomes a habit in your mind. Take on the power of Stoicism and use it to lead a happier and more meaningful life than before.

Chapter 5

Develop Unbreakable Emotional Intelligence

C R Jung said, 'Everything that annoys us about other people helps us understand ourselves better.' To reiterate something that has been said before in this book, Stoics are not unemotional, unfeeling people. They feel happy and sad, get hurt when someone says nasty things to them, and identify with all emotions that non-Stoics connect with.

The difference between Stoics and non-Stoics is that the Stoics know and understand the importance of managing and handling their emotions. They do not suppress emotions, and instead, channelize the power of feelings to live life well, which in turn results in a peaceful, happy life. Stoics are students of everything human, including emotions.

The biggest challenge for Stoics is to learn in accordance with nature. Nature does not include only the positive but the negatives too. The messy and strange interactions of life are all part of nature, and we cannot avoid them. Stoics accept that emotions are part of human life. Therefore, it is wise to embrace them and leverage their power to the best extent possible. However, it is important not to give excess power to emotions.

Emotional Intelligence

Stoics have a distinctive approach to emotions, which makes them emotionally intelligent and strong. Stoics know that to be guided by emotions is a foolhardy thing to do. On the contrary, emotions are to be treated like the weather that keeps changing depending on various factors.

For example, during rainy weather, you must drive slowly and carry an umbrella while walking. During a storm, don't we stay indoors to protect ourselves? Similarly, when emotions are low or during an emotional storm, it is best not to take decisions or even avoid talking to people until the storm blows over.

Moreover, you cannot use emotions as an excuse to behave badly with other people. For example, if you said something rude to your colleagues or your teammates, and then explained your behavior by saying, 'Because it was raining.' Wouldn't that be considered weird by people? Stoics believe that behaving like a jerk when you are angry is equally weird, obnoxious, and nonsensical.

Stoics believe that emotions are invariably a result of wrong or misplaced perceptions. Also, Stoics strongly opine that everyone has the option of behaving virtuously regardless of the external circumstances. Therefore, emotional management is a crucial aspect of Stoicism.

Dealing with Emotions Stoically

Stoicism recognizes three 'good feelings' contrasting with three 'bad feelings.' The three good emotions referred to as *hai eupatheia*i in Greek are caution, joy, and wish. The bad feelings contrasting to these three good emotions are fear, pleasure, and lust. Therefore,

Stoic philosophy has the following set of emotions defined:

- ❖ Caution Vs. Fear
- ❖ Joy Vs. Pleasure
- ❖ Wish Vs. Lust

Let us try and understand why the ancient Stoics decided to focus on these emotions. First, nearly all other emotions can be categorized into one or more of these overarching types. Now, let us take wish, and see why Stoics called a wish a good feeling and lust (sometimes the word appetite is also used) as a bad feeling.

The reason is actually easy to understand from a Stoic perspective. Being lustful or having an appetite is pining for things that you cannot or do not have, and this approach is a total waste of time and energy, according to the Stoics. For example, greed is an appetite for material things; enmity is an appetite that feeds the idea of revenge, etc.

Emotions like greed and enmity burn up our energy and time resources on fantasies driving us to do unproductive work. Remember that Stoics don't waste their resources on things they cannot control. Fantasies are uncontrollable elements, and therefore, any emotion that feeds fantasies are to be avoided as bad feelings.

As per Stoic philosophy, a wish goes something like this, 'I wish I could have access to more money. However, my happiness is not based on the realization of this wish.' Appetite, on the other hand, says that if things around me get better, then I will be happy.

Therefore, a wish is something that is based on the core principles of Stoicism, which is, 'virtue is the only good, and the only thing we can control is our actions.' Having wishes is a fertile ground to grow and expand wisdom.

Caution vs. fear works on similar ideas. Fear is an irrational avoidance to an imagined or real danger. Fear is an emotion that takes away the joy of the present moment by compelling us to focus on some event that may or may not happen in the future. Contrarily, caution teaches us that challenges and obstacles will come in our way, and it is wise to prepare ourselves to face them or avoid them if possible. Yet, peace of mind and happiness is not based on external things. Stoicism teaches us to face the world with awareness and not with fear.

Tips to Build Emotional Intelligence - Here are some tips that can help you build emotional intelligence with which you can lead a happier and more contented life than before.

The Stoic Triangle of Happiness

The Stoic Triangle of Happiness consists of three elements at each of the vortexes and eudaimonia or flourishing life in the middle. The elements at the three corners of the triangle are taking responsibility, focusing on what you can control, and living with arete. When you combine these three elements of Stoicism, you get to experience eudaimonia. Let us look at each of the three corners in a bit of detail.

Live with arete - This corner of the triangle stands for living at your full potential at all times. Performing at your best potential means, you have to continually reduce the gap between what you are capable of and your current performance. In the modern world, Abraham Maslow spoke about self-actualization, which is nothing but living your life to your best capability.

Arete in Greek means 'excellence.' Arete is the highest quality of life you can lead. When you strive to live with arete, you are endeavoring to get the best quality of every work that you do. Instead of being anxious about your feelings while doing a task, you must focus your energies to do your best. Typically, when you have to do something to avoid the question, 'How will this make me feel?' Instead, ask yourself this question, 'What can I do to make sure my best capabilities are being put to use in this task?'

The more you live with arete, the more your capabilities increase. Understanding the concept of arete is easy. However, implementing the concept in your life can take an entire lifetime. Stoics only endeavor to live with arete at all times. They falter time and again. But they don't hesitate to get up and try again and again.

Discontentment is likely to brew when there is a gap between your highest self and your current level of living. Therefore, Stoics are always finding ways to close this gap as much as possible so that they are able to live in arete.

Focus on what you can control - This vortex of the Stoic Triangle of Happiness is the cornerstone of Stoicism. Stoics are strong believers of focusing on what you can control and accepting everything that cannot be controlled. You can achieve eudaimonia if you choose to behave and act responsibly regardless of the external uncontrollable factors. The biggest challenge to focus on what you can control is to stop worrying about things that you cannot control. Here are some useful suggestions for you:

First, identify what you can control - Take any given situation, and list out the factors that influence it. Now, identify all the things that you can control. Here are some examples:

- ❖ You cannot prevent the coming of a storm. But, you can prepare yourself for it.

❖ You cannot control the actions of other people. But, you can control how you react/respond to them.

Focus on your area of influence - You can influence circumstances and people. However, you cannot always get the outcome of your choice. For example, you can do everything in your power to make sure the party you plan turns out well. However, you cannot influence people to have fun.

Similarly, you can give your child everything he or she needs to do well in school. You could buy the best of books, get the best of tutors to teach him, etc. However, whether your child will get a 4.0 CGPA is not under your control.

Therefore, identify the areas that you can influence and focus on these areas. Stop worrying about elements that are outside the area of your influence. Most importantly, focus on altering your behaviors to bring about positive changes in your life.

Identify and tackle your fears - What is it that you are afraid of? Are you worried that a catastrophic outcome will take place? Do you doubt your capabilities to handle it? Are you scared of facing disappointments in your life?

Ask yourself various questions and use the answers you get to identify your fears. Once you identify them, then you can find ways to overcome them. Typically, the worst case scenario is not as bad as you imagined it to be. Most often, you realize that you are stronger than what you thought yourself to be.

For example, if you are worried about your business failing, then you can prepare yourself for the bad situation. When you realize that you can handle the worst case scenario, then you are likely to feel motivated and charged up to get things done.

Know the difference between problem-solving and ruminating over problems - Repeating a worst case scenario is ruminating, whereas working out solutions for potential problems is problem-solving. Know the difference between the two and avoid ruminating over problems. Instead, focus on problem-solving, and you will realize it is easy to keep your mind on things you can control and let go of things you cannot control.

Take responsibility - The third corner of the Stoic Triangle of Happiness is to take responsibility. You are entirely responsible for your life because every external factor that influences your life has one component you can control, which is how you choose to respond to the external factors. Stoicism teaches us that the external circumstances themselves have little or no influence on our happiness or miserable. What makes us miserable or happiness is how we interpret the external situations. Here are some suggestions to help you take responsibility for your life:

Assume responsibility for your feelings, thoughts, and actions - You are part of all these three aspects of human interaction. Your thoughts are coming from your mind, your feelings are coming from your life experiences, and your actions are coming from your physical body. Nobody can make you feel, think, or do anything without your approval.

Avoid blaming people and complaining about things - Stop blaming people and circumstances for the things happening in your life. Blaming your parents, spouse, country, or your upbringing for your misfortunes will not help you in any way.

When you blame people, you take on the role of victim. When you take responsibility for yourself, you become the victor. With this approach, you can choose the best route available to you. Complaining is also a form of playing a victim role. Therefore, stop complaining and do what you can do.

Don't take anything personally - Don't take anything personally in your life. Taking disagreements as being a personal attack on you is foolhardy. Most often, things are not about you personally. It is more about issues. Even if you have a doubt, it is best to ask questions and clarify your doubts instead of taking things personally.

The Stoic Triangle of Happiness helps to break down the Stoic philosophical points into easy-to-understand and easy-to-follow practice tips so that everyone can implement these ideas into their daily life.

Negative Visualization

Negative visualization is a Stoic practice that has come down through the ages. It has helped many people become mentally strong and overcome even the hardest challenges in their lives with ease. Have you ever thought of the worst thing that can happen to you? Tough thing to do, right?

However, negative visualization has multiple benefits and is a powerful Stoic tool to help you cope with the most difficult aspects of your life smoothly. Stoicism believes that while you can take precautions to avoid or overcome negativity in your life, you are unlikely to be completely free from encountering negativity and challenges. No matter how hard you try to avoid them, some bad things are bound to come your way. Being mentally prepared to handle these bad things is crucial to living a life of meaning and happiness. Negative visualization is a tool that helps you in this regard.

What is negative visualization? When you are getting ready to do some big task, you must voluntarily visualize bad outcomes and scenarios that are likely to happen. When you practice negative visualizations, you become mentally prepared to handle bad situations when they actually occur.

Stoics mentally train themselves to live virtuously. They understand that it is easy to be virtuous when life is smooth and happens as per your wish. However, the aim of Stoicism is to lead a virtuous life irrespective of the external circumstances. So, even when the external situation is unpleasant, we must train ourselves to live virtuously. Negative visualization techniques help in this regard.

Negative visualization referred to as *premeditatio malorum* which translates to 'foreseeing bad stuff,' is a tool that trains your mind to think and imagine bad situations and learn to stay calm, composed, and free from the influence of negative emotions during difficult times.

The reason why negative situations are imagined is to reiterate to practicing Stoics that external circumstances by themselves are indifferent. Our reactions to them are what makes them positive or negative. Negative visualization trains our mind to respond smartly to negativism-triggering external situations.

How to practice negative visualization - Negative visualization is the opposite of postmortem, where the doctor tries to find out the cause of death after a person dies. In negative visualization, we look at scenarios that can potentially cause death and find ways to manage the impending negative situation when it actually happens. So, negative visualization can help you prevent a death-like situation to become a reality.

Let us take a job interview scenario and apply negative visualization techniques to help you overcome potential problems. Use the following steps:

- ❖ Imagine the worst things that can go wrong in the interview. Don't hesitate to let your imagination go wild, and think of all the things that can go wrong before or during the interview.
- ❖ Visualize these negative things like as if they are happening right now, and not in the future.

- ❖ Now, even when you imagine negative scenarios, your body is likely to react strongly. Remember to stay calm right through the visualization process.
- ❖ Think of the things you can do during such a situation. Come out with solutions for the impending problems and make sure you get yourself prepared to handle such situations if they were to actually happen.

You can use the above steps in any given scenario to help you manage negative solutions. Being practical and preparing yourself for the worst case scenario is not a pessimistic attitude. In fact, it is a highly optimistic approach because, despite the fear of so many things that can go wrong, you are ready to take the plunge. Therefore, negative visualization practiced by Stoics does not make people pessimists It just trains their body and mind to respond smartly even in the most adverse of situations.

Stoic Exercises to Build Self-Awareness and Mindfulness

Self-reflection is a key element to help you identify your traits and increase your self-awareness. Use the following Stoic practices to help you in this regard:

Indulge in early morning reflection - The Stoic exercise of self-reflection in the morning goes beyond making to-do lists. It involves preparing your body and mind with negative visualization techniques. Visualize the expected problems of the upcoming day, and plan how you are going to respond to them.

Remind yourself each morning of this timeless quote from Seneca, 'Don't give in to adversity, don't trust prosperity and wealth, and know that fortune changes hands as she pleases.' When you go prepared with the idea that you are your only true friend, then your resolve is strengthened to get through the obstacles of the day.

Don't forget to show gratitude during your morning self-reflection ritual. Be thankful for getting to live another day. Many people in the world don't get this privilege. Check your schedule for the day, and make plans as to how you are going to embrace virtues and discard vices. And finally, don't forget to remind yourself that the only things under your control are your attitude, behavior, and reactions.

Other thoughts you can contemplate on are:

- ❖ Meditate on how you can improve yourself to become a better human being.
- ❖ Contemplate on your death and on the fact that you are bound to age.

Take a bird's eye view of your life - This exercise is meant to remind you of how small and insignificant our life is in comparison to the vastness of this world. Here is a simple practice you can try:

Sit in a quiet, undisturbed place.

Imagine looking at yourself from the clouds. See how small you look. In fact, you may not even be visible if you were to hover from the clouds and look down.

Slowly zoom into your world, and watch everything getting bigger and bigger until you can see yourself sitting and meditating.

Now, zoom out of yourself and imagine going upwards. Watch everything getting smaller and smaller as you move further high up into the sky.

Imagine yourself in space, looking at the expanding vastness of space.

As you watch the world coming towards you and going away from you, watch everything that is happening non-judgmentally. Look at the wars, parties, famines, floods, and everything else that is taking place in the world objectively. This exercise will remind you that many things that you have been holding as being very important are only mildly important in your own life.

This exercise helps you discern the controllable and uncontrollable aspects of your life. When you become aware of the things that are truly important in your life, then you can focus your energies primarily on those elements resulting in improved productivity and efficiency.

Create an ideal person in your imagination - This exercise is designed to help you make progress towards becoming a better human being. Being an ideal human being is not really possible in this world, believe the Stoics. However, we can continuously progress towards self-improvement.

Visualize the elements that make an ideal human being. Think of the Greek and Roman statues that depict perfection in physical form. Imagine people who are so deeply compassionate towards other people that they are willing to sacrifice even their lives for others.

Create a list of role models you have in mind. Think of all the good qualities that they possess and which you want to copy. Don't dwell excessively on the negative qualities of your role model. Remember, everyone is trying to achieve idealism. No one in the human world has yet reached the state of sagehood.

Alternately, you can contemplate on the worst kind of human being and think of all their characteristics. This exercise is to wake you up to the things you must avoid doing.

Cultivate the habit of giving - The art of philanthropy is not excluded to the donation of wealth and money. In Stoic terms, the art of giving is based on bringing as many people as close to yourself as possible. This can happen if you put everyone you meet under your umbrella of kindness and compassion.

Remember that you have to be suspicious of your own opinions and thoughts until you are sure of their correctness. And you have to be sympathetic towards others' opinions and thoughts before being suspicious. That is a core principle of Stoicism. Practicing Stoic philanthropy is nothing but taking everyone along with you and not treating anyone with disrespect.

Of course, if you are a wealthy Stoic, philanthropy in the form of donating money is also a welcome Stoic sign. The important thing is to cultivate the habit of giving and not hoarding.

Retreat into your mind as often as possible - Most people in modern times choose to travel the world as a way of self-reflection and self-retreat and to find peace of mind. In fact, taking off on a trip was a fad even during the times of the ancient Greeks. However, there is an alternative that is more effective to find peace and calm.

Marcus Aurelius said, 'Why should you travel to the hillside or the seashore for peace of mind when it is possible to retreat into your inner self regardless of where you are? There is no better place for peace than the seat of your own soul. When you are going through stress, all you need to do is look at the root of your problem and emotions, and you will get relief and peace of mind.'

The Stoics believe that peace and happiness are available within us and not outside of us. Therefore, traveling may not be a very effective way for this. Instead, travel inside your mind. Every day for about 10 minutes, shut out the outside world, close your eyes, and look deep inside your heart and mind. Each time you retreat into your heart and mind, you will cleanse yourself of distress and return to the world refreshed and rejuvenated to take on the challenges of life with renewed vigor.

While initially, it is possible to practice self-retreat only in a calm, undisturbed place, it makes sense to keep trying to get into your mind even in crowded and noisy places. The more you practice this exercise, the easier it gets to turn inward whenever you feel like it.

Strip away layers from any given situation that causes stress - The human mind loves complications. Therefore, it adds layers of information, data, and other undue elements to any given situation to complicate and confuse you. The core issue of the matter gets lost in these unimportant layers. Whenever you feel depressed, distressed, or upset about any given situation, find answers to the following questions:

- ❖ What good is this situation, and what would be the potential response for me and other people? Almost always, the answer to this question will be 'no good at all.'
- ❖ If the situation is really worth getting stressed out, then what are the qualities that are needed to overcome it? If you are already qualified, then use your abilities and sort out the problem.

Else, work on developing these qualities so that you are prepared for the next time.

Therefore, before making any decisions about any given situation, strip away all the layers that cover the core issue, and focus on solving the primary problem. You will not only conserve time and energy but also come up with excellent and sustainable solutions for the problem.

Stoicism emphasized the importance of emotional intelligence a couple of millennia before the modern psychologists even thought of a term to describe emotional management. Using Stoic principles to manage your emotions will help you make sensible, prudent life decisions aligned with your nature.

Chapter 6

THE PREPARATION YOU NEED FOR MODERN DAY LIFE

Although the philosophy of Stoicism was created more than 2000 years ago, its tenets and principles continue to be relevant to this day. Let us who you can prepare yourself with these tenets and morals so that you can lead a fulfilling, meaningful life in the modern world. The Stoic practices mentioned in this chapter will help you maintain calm even in the face of the diversity of the chaotic outside world.

Identify Your Inner Control Center

Epictetus said, 'Our frustration and pains are not rooted in the external circumstances but in our own reactions and responses to external stimuli. Nearly all of what happens to us is not under our influence or control. This undeniable truth is the foundation on which Stoicism was founded.

Realizing this powerful truth helped Stoics to find ways to focus only on the elements that are directly under their control or influence. Epictetus himself was born a slave, and what he had under his control was, perhaps, far, far less than what you and I have influence over in the modern world. And yet, he managed to live a happy, meaningful life, and his works and writings continue to inspire people even after two millennia.

Epictetus told himself that he would use the things under his control wisely. The things that Epictetus had control over were his desires, opinions, likes, and dislikes. No one could take away control of these elements from him. He used the power of his influence over these matters and ensured he lived a good, morally upright life, an example that is valid even today!

The modern world is replete with elements that frustrate and annoy you. The technological and economic advancements of modern life have made us so comfortable that the slightest inconvenience irritates us. The Internet is one of the fastest things invented today. And yet, if the response of a web page could even a second longer than what we are used to, we are angered and annoyed.

During such times of frustration, recall Stoicism. Remember that the cause of the annoyance may be the speed of the Internet, which you cannot control. But the choice to get annoyed is under your control. Use this center of control and find ways not to be angry or irritated in the given situation.

The choice to not let external circumstances dictate your emotional response is under your direct control. Find that inner center of control, and make sure you hold the keys to it. Then, you will find it easy to manage your emotions, and consequently, your responses regardless of the external stimuli.

Remember that we don't control any event that is happening to us or around us. But, we control what these events mean to us. Find this locus of control to find the power of a Stoic life.

Time is Precious

The ancient Stoics were truly wise people. The most precious commodity for them was not wealth, money, or property. It was time! Time is the only thing in this world that which is lost will never be recovered ever again. The Stoics appreciated the value of this highly limited resource. Therefore, Stoics strive hard not to waste this precious resource.

In the modern world, multiple time-consuming technology-based distractions vie for your attention. It is imperative that you become wary of the amount of time you spend on these wasteful activities. We get so caught up with mindless internet browsing, scrolling through oodles of information on social media platforms, and other such activities that we procrastinate important work because of the lack of time.

We keep putting things off for tomorrow that might never come. Therefore, make sure you maintain your timetable and stick to your schedule so that you don't waste time needlessly. Of course, it makes sense to allocate some amount of time for leisure too, which could include browsing through your favorite social media platform or anything else of your choice.

Another way we lose time is by spending too much of it on others without completing our own important tasks. Be wary of fulfilling needless obligations for other people so much so that you put off your own work. This is also a form of wasting time. Committing yourself without thinking is also to be included in this category. Learn to say no when you are aware that what is being asked of you will take away unnecessary time.

Regardless of what work you do, time is of the essence, and make sure you don't waste this precious resource.

Your Happiness is Your Responsibility

Most of us love ourselves more than we love anybody else. And yet, we choose to demean ourselves and our opinions to the point that we begin to think we are not good enough for the world. Avoid falling into this trap. Remember, you can be happy only if you choose to be so. Your happiness is your responsibility. Don't outsource the task of keeping yourself happy to someone else. They are bound to make a mess of it.

To be happy with yourself, avoid looking for other people's approval. You don't need anyone's approval to be happy. You don't need to spend money to buy fancy clothes, jewels, gadgets, or anything else to be happy. Have you realized how much time, money, and effort it takes to get the approval of others? Instead, if you simply choose to be content with your lot, you will be happy, and no one can distract you from your path of happiness.

Ask yourself if you have chosen a career or lifestyle because it matters to other people in your life. Have you chosen to be an engineer instead of being a musician because the trend in society was to be an engineer? Did you or did you not choose your career because it is the best option for you?

Don't allow yourself to be held hostage and pay an exorbitant price for it. Moreover, the more you pay, the less chance you have of getting free from the grasp of having to please others to be happy. You are more likely to be taken for granted, and an increasing number of people will use you to find their happiness, leaving you completely wrecked and bone-dry of joy.

Take control of your happiness, and choose your life according to what is best for you.

Be Wary of Distractions

The modern world is filled with innumerable options, and taking the time and effort to make your choice can be a mind-boggling exercise. In fact, the excessive number of options has not really benefited us. Instead, it has drained our energy as we struggle each day, trying to make the best choices for ourselves. There is an overpowering amount of information available and gleaning through this huge amount of data to find what is good for us, we end up wasting a lot of time and effort on this exercise.

Also, having so many options distract us to the point that we are scared of committing ourselves to one path. We put off decisions, or worse still, pursue multiple things simultaneously resulting in procrastination or quality-compromised work. Therefore, Stoicism warns us about being distracted unnecessarily from our primary motive of life, which is being virtuous and living according to nature.

Stoics know and understand the disruptions to your peace and serenity will happen. The trick is finding ways to accept these disruptions as being part of the natural way of things. So, Stoics believe in taking purposeful action instead of reacting continuously to the myriad external stimuli attracting us towards them.

Eliminate Vanity and Ego from Your Life

Epictetus said, 'Throw out all your conceited thoughts and opinions because you cannot learn anything if you believe that you already know everything.' Even as a teacher, one of the biggest challenges that Epictetus faced was to teach students who think they have come to learn but also believe that they know almost everything there is to know.

There is nothing but vanity and ego at the heart of such thoughts. This kind of I-know-all attitude is highly dangerous, especially in the modern day when things change overnight. Marcus Aurelius said that the universe is a change whereas human life is an opinion. And in the modern world where things are changing at an extremely rapid pace, this attitude can be your nemesis.

The vast amount of information available at our fingertips can actually be a deterrent rather than helping us make informed choices. We are continually disrupted by changing opinions, ideas, thoughts, and discoveries. That is the reason why most wise men in the modern world spend a significant portion of their time reading and gaining knowledge.

It makes sense to take a leaf out of such wise people's books, throw out vanity and ego, and always be a humble student of the universe.

Stand Firm on Your Principles

The modern world is built on the basis of compromises. It might seem to the casual observer. This statement might be true to some extent. And yet, there have been men and women who have had the courage to stand firm on their principles in the face of the most devious devices that tried to break them. And Stoics are made of such strong stuff.

Stoicism teaches no gray areas. Virtues are all good and have the same quality of goodness. Vices are all bad and have the same intensity of evil. The modern world where it seems that the pendulum of compromise has swung too far for much good, Stoicism is a breath of fresh air in terms of such uncompromising stances.

While standing firm on your principles might come across as unreasonable for the uninitiated, it is only a matter of time when you realize the power of an uncompromising stand. When you are firm on your principles and choose to remain inflexible, you are empowered with an unshakable authority that will help you increase your Stoic behavior.

Such powerful behavior is likely to motivate others to stand on their principles, and slowly but surely, the world will undergo a positive change with regard to a moral and virtuous life. A compromised world might be a thing of the past if all of us choose to stand firm on our values.

Nothing in the World is Permanent

Marcus Aurelius wrote, 'Alexander the Great died, and so did his mule driver. Both met with the same end.'

In the grand scheme of things in the universe, our achievements, no matter how big they seem, relegate into nothingness. This concept is not only a sobering thought but also keeps us grounded to reality. Most of us experience a feeling that we are the center of the universe, which ends up inflating our ego and making us vain. When we realize that even the most powerful of the world emperors and kings died just like a slave did, we experience humility.

Everything and everyone around us is impermanent. The most brilliant of minds like Newton, Edison,

Abraham Lincoln, Churchill, Gandhi, and many, many more people are nothing more than footnotes today. We will meet the same fate too. Of course, our names might not even make footnotes in any book.

The realization of the impermanence aspect of nature and the universe is a humbling thought, and we must continually remind ourselves of this powerful truth. Then, we will not feel vanity by our achievements or excessive depression from our failures. We will have the resolve to take both pain and pleasure with equanimity.

Moreover, this truth helps us from feeling compelled to live life in conformity of other people. It frees us from having to mindlessly chase accomplishments because we realize that nothing lasts forever. The only thing worthy of following is to live a good, virtuous life.

Create Disruptions in Your Life

Another effective way to learn to manage distractions is by creating disruptions. How will you do this? Keep finding ways to move out of your comfort zone, and get comfortable with the uncomfortable.

When we operate out of habit, we run things on autopilot, and we stop thinking and deliberating about our decisions and our actions. We begin to live life mindlessly in our comfort zone. So, to remain mindful of our life, actions, and thoughts, creating disruptions and making things uncomfortable for ourselves works very well. Use these suggestions to create disruptions and learn to get comfortable with the uncomfortable:

Take the first step - When you are planning to start something new, the first step is always the most difficult one. When you want to start running instead of walking, taking that first step to start running is the trickiest part. When you have taken that first step, then the others will follow automatically.

Similarly, starting a diet to lose weight is always a problem. Once you've got through the first day of the day, you will find it easy to do the second day, and so forth. Therefore, if you choose to do something outside of your comfort zone, don't waste time on excessive analysis. Just start the venture.

Don't give up easily - So, you have started on something uncomfortable. But, the path is more difficult than you thought. The feeling of discomfort is increasing instead of decreasing. Don't panic and give up your endeavor. Just persist until the positive changes take place. Remember, the harder it gets, the more power you are gaining by fighting it. So, don't give up easily.

Push yourself beyond your comfort zone - Many times, we say to ourselves, 'I have never done this before. I am not certain if I will ever be able to do this well.' When you have such thoughts, you know you have reached the limits of your current comfort zone. Recognize it, and push yourself beyond this point.

Go ahead, and accept to do the activity you have never done before. A significant portion of our dreams is killed because of fear and uncertainty. Fake self-confidence if you need to, at least initially. As you progress in your effort, the self-confidence will turn to genuine. Remember that fear kills far more dreams than failure.

Embrace the problems in your life - You know that some aspects of your life suck and the problems in that area never seem to go away. Don't try to drive away that part of your life. On the contrary, embrace it and welcome it like an old friend. When you behave in this way, your mindset will change, and you will see perspectives that remained hidden until now. Consequently, the chances of finding sustainable solutions for these problems increase.

Identify the areas you have improved in - As you train yourself to become comfortable with the uncomfortable, you will see improvements in multiple areas of your life. Identify these areas and be proud of your achievements. Of course, you must remember to use your pride to motivate yourself to do better. It should never be allowed to stray into the realm of vanity.

So, go ahead and start creating disruptions in your life so that you are ever ready to deal with the challenges that life throws at you.

You Always Have a Choice

Regardless of your status and position in society, whether in good times or bad, or in the presence of any external stimuli, remember you always have a choice. You could be in prison, or you could be the CEO of a successful company. The choices you make in that position are completely under your control.

The society has a wide range of hierarchies. Some of us are extremely poor, and some of us are abominably rich. We come from varied backgrounds experiencing the highs and lows of life. At every stage, we have a choice to do, say, and behave the way we want to. According to Stoicism, this freedom of choice is a sign of liberty. No matter how hard life seems at present, this freedom of choice is what will free us from suffering.

Always Look Inwards

Look at these scenarios:

- ❖ Noticing the beat of your favorite song playing vs. noticing your heart beat faster when your crush walks past you.
- ❖ Noticing the amazing aroma of freshly baked bread vs. noticing you are breathing very hard.

All four observation exercises require paying attention, right? However, noticing your heartbeat and observing your breath requires you to pay attention to your inner self, whereas the other two require you to pay attention to the external surroundings.

Most of us are preconditioned to focusing our attention on external surroundings. We focus on our work, TV, gadgets, conversations with friends, etc. However, there is an entire vista of scenery available within our body. These include our feelings, the way we breathe, the way our heart beats, and many more sensations and emotions.

And it is this internal world that decides whether we should be happy or sad, angry or hurt, etc. When we control and manage this internal world of sensations correctly, we can be happy even when stuck in the middle of horrific traffic. When we don't have control of this inner world, we can be angry, sad, and resentful even in the midst of beautiful surroundings.

Stoics are always finding time and energy to look inwards at their own hearts and souls to see what is happening. They look inwards when things go wrong, and they look inwards when things go right too. Looking inwards is a powerful tool for self-improvement. Moreover, it helps you control your choices based on your needs and not be moved or get carried away by external circumstances.

Nearly all the answers for your life questions are inside of you. Therefore, it is imperative that you take every opportunity to look within and find those answers. You have to be brutally honest with yourself during the period of self-contemplation. Of course, avoid being brutal and cruel to yourself. Remind yourself that everyone starts at some point, and this is yours!

When you turn inwards, you find your anxiety is soothed, and you feel an increased sense of wellbeing. Consequently, you find the resolve and strength needed to live a happy life despite humongous challenges bothering you.

Avoid Fear and Paranoia

Nearly all our imagined fears are far, far more brutal than reality. However, this imagination can wreak havoc on your state of mind. Therefore, it is important to manage fear and not allow it to destroy your ability to be happy. If you let fear control you, then it means you are not in control of your choices. Here are some suggestions on how to manage fear:

Sit with your fears for a couple of minutes - Before you choose to react to your fears, just sit with them for a couple of minutes. Observe the thoughts in your mind as fear passes through your body and mind. Talk to your fears, 'It is ok, don't worry.' Tell yourself that emotions ebb and flow like the waves in the ocean.

Do something to distract yourself from the fear - When you have regained your composure, do something that will further distract you from your fears. Get engaged in an activity. Paint, color, draw, listen to music or talk to a dear friend. Do something enjoyable that is easy for you to get immersed in.

Recall the things you are grateful - When you see things that bring you happiness and joy and for which you feel gratitude, fear is bound to take a backseat.

Use humor - Read, listen to, or watch something funny. It could be your favorite comedy show or a funny movie. Laughter is a great tool to reduce anxiety pangs.

Fear is a debilitating emotion that can jeopardize not only your life but also that of the people around you, including your loved ones. Moreover, when you are afraid, the fearful thoughts will project themselves on others, and wittingly or unwittingly, they will give you what you feared the most. Manage your fear before it controls you and your life.

Stoicism is an effective philosophy for the modern day. The concepts and ideas it teaches have been around for centuries and have been tried and tested by many people throughout the history of mankind. It would be naive not to try out a few Stoic-based strategies and recommendations to prepare for and live well in the modern world.

Chapter 7

INTRODUCING A DAILY STOIC ROUTINE

Now that you know the power of being a Stoic, it makes sense to put Stoic-based practices into your daily life. This chapter provides you some aids, tips, and suggestions for a daily Stoic routine.

Morning Stoic Ritual

Marcus Aurelius said, 'When you wake up each morning, tell yourself that you are going to meet with crazy people, liars, cheats, busybodies, and many more varieties of people throughout the day. The thing with these negative people is that they don't know the difference between virtue and vice.'

One of the most popular and established Stoic routines is self-reflection. The best time for this exercise as advocated by Stoics is in the morning as soon as you wake up and at night just before you go to bed. During the morning self-reflection time, you must rehearse the events and experiences of the day, and before going to bed, you must review the experiences and events that happened during the day. Some of the questions to contemplate in your morning session are:

- ❖ What are the things I still don't have to be free from the effects of negative emotions?
- ❖ What should I do to achieve peace and tranquility?
- ❖ What should I do to make my behavior align with my nature, which is that of a rational, thinking being?

The reasoning behind these questions is becoming increasingly better each day. It is a core Stoic principle to continuously endeavor to become a better person each day. When you repeatedly search for answers to these questions, you are learning new things about yourself and about Stoicism each day, and your knowledge and self-awareness are getting a big boost.

The question on rational being is to remind yourself of your nature, which is not to be overly attached to external things. The purpose of the morning reflection is to increasingly aspire for improved virtuous living and better reasoning capabilities. Marcus Aurelius said that we are duty-bound to feel grateful for being alive each morning. We should give thanks to the universe for the fact that we can breathe, live, eat, and enjoy another day in this world.

The morning ritual should also contain negative visualization exercises so that you feel prepared to meet and overcome the challenges of the day head-on. The trick is in preparing to meet negative people and circumstances with love, compassion, patience, and forgiveness. It is important to remember that negative visualization is not to go against the world but to find your peace in a chaotic world.

The morning time is also to remind ourselves about the impermanence of everything which, in turn, should increase our intensity of gratitude. You must remind yourself that whatever you have earned in the last few years can be destroyed in a few seconds by nature. Nothing is permanent. Recall how large cities and towns were swallowed up in minutes by natural disasters like earthquakes and tsunamis. All these reflections remind you repeatedly that you are mortal, and that the only thing worth working for is to live a good, moral life.

Stoics strongly believe that a morning ritual is essential if you have to remain calm and peaceful when storms strike. You can alter this morning routine to fit your lifestyle. You could choose to meditate over these ideas or think of them while you go for your morning exercises or contemplate on thoughts of Stoicism when you have a shower.

Just remember to remind yourself of your mortality each morning, and show gratitude to the universe for another new day.

Meditation

Meditation is the art of exercising your mind, similar to sports being the art of training your body. There are multiple benefits of meditation, including:

- ❖ It keeps you healthy by lowering blood pressure, cholesterol, and many other health-related factors.
- ❖ Lowers heart rate, which helps you calm down and feel at peace.
- ❖ You feel less anxious and stressed out.
- ❖ You find an increased sense of wellbeing.

Use the following steps to start meditating. This simple breathing exercise can be categorized as mindful breathing also.

- ❖ Sit or lie down comfortably.
- ❖ Close your eyes.
- ❖ Don't try to control your breath. Just breathe normally.
- ❖ Focus on your breath and pay attention to how your body is moving as you inhale and exhale. Observe your chest heaving, stomach moving, and the hot and cold air blowing in and out of your nostrils as you breathe.
- ❖ Your thoughts are likely to move off to something else like the work that you need to do once you finish your meditation session.

Follow your thoughts, and then gently bring back your attention to your breath.

Every time your thoughts wander, bring them back to your breath. Remember not to be frustrated with the exercise because our mind is like a monkey jumping from one thought to another before you can catch it. Don't try to control your thoughts. Instead, follow them, and then slowly train your mind to focus on your breath.

Mastering this technique can take several days, or perhaps even months. Be patient with yourself and persist. The benefits are many, and you will find it worth your efforts. Start small and take baby steps. Don't think of meditating for one hour a day on the first day. You are likely to give up on Day 1 itself.

Look at meditating or sitting still for 5 minutes each day trying to focus on your breath. Slowly increase the duration by another 5 minutes after a week or so. Take your time and don't be in a hurry to do a long stretch of meditation at once. Your mind is used to jumping around, and you will have to be patient until it has learned to become still. Just persist at meditation, and even if you cannot achieve 30 minutes at a stretch, you will find that you are getting multiple benefits.

Mindfulness

Mindfulness is one of the biggest paradoxes in the human world, considering that the theory is very simple to understand but extremely difficult to practice. For example, suppose you were to sit on a beach and watch the sun setting in the horizon. You watch and hear the lapping of the water, the reddish orange color of the setting sun scattering across the sky, and for a few unbroken seconds, you practice mindfulness completely immersed in the peaceful moment.

Now, imagine a situation where you are grieving the loss of a loved one. The pain is so great that all you want to do is to forget about it. You would want to do everything in your power to get rid of the agonizing pain of loss. Mindfulness calls for you to immerse yourself completely in this kind of pain. Would you be able to do that as easily as you enjoyed the scene of the setting sun?

However, mindfulness can be practiced starting with beautiful moments and slowly moving on the painful moments. Cultivating mindfulness is one of the most basic tenets of Stoicism. The more mindful you become, the more self-awareness you build, and consequently, you will find yourself leading a happier and more fulfilling life than before. Here are some basic tips when you start the practice of mindfulness.

Start with simple things - For example, focus on the sensations on your lips, mouth, and throat as you take cool sips of water when you are thirsty. When you hug your baby, be aware of the warm sensation of love and affection awakening within you. At your next meal, focus on the flavors of the dishes you are eating. A section below is dedicated to mindful eating.

You can practice mindfulness with any activity you do - Mindfulness is not just about sitting quietly for an hour at a stretch and observing your breath. You can practice mindfulness in any of your daily activities. Here are some activities you can start immediately.

Mindful eating - Reflect on the eating habits of modern life. Most of us eat lunch at our desk, trying to complete an email or some other task. Dinner is usually in front of the TV. We don't even realize what we are eating, how it tastes (unless it is high-sugar or high salt content), or anything else about the food. This approach is the exact opposite of mindful eating. Practice mindful eating with the following steps:

- ❖ Sit at the dining table, and make sure you are not multitasking your meal with any other work.
- ❖ Keep your mobile and other electronic devices silent or switched off.
- ❖ Look at the plate of food and pay attention to the different items on it. Focus on the color and shape of the food.
- ❖ Take a small bite and put it in your mouth. Feel it with your tongue, and then start chewing. It is recommended that you chew every mouthful 20 times.
- ❖ As you chew your food, focus on the taste, texture, and flavor of what you are eating.

- ❖ See if you can recognize the ingredients that have gone into making the dish.
- ❖ Remember to take the next bite only when you completely swallowed the previous bite.

This way of eating might seem like a waste of mind for the novice, mindful practitioners. However, persist at it, and you will realize multiple benefits of mindful eating, including prevention of overeating, resetting of your taste buds, healthy meal options, and more. In fact, as you continue to practice mindful eating, you can go further down the journey of your food. You can think of how the ingredient was grown, harvested, cleaned, milled, packed, and transported to your place. Mindful eating also helps you become conscious of how complex the process of bringing food to your table is.

Mindful walking - Most of us walk for health reasons, and nearly all of us walk only because we have to, and not because we want to. Mindful walking can help you change your idea about the skill of walking. Next time you walk on the road or anywhere else, use the following tips:

- ❖ Pay attention to your feet as you lift each foot to move forward.
- ❖ Feel the pressure of walking on your calf muscles, thighs, and hips.
- ❖ Feel the movement of your hips as you move forward.
- ❖ Pay attention to the movement of your arms as you swing them.
- ❖ Focus on the beating of your heart and your breathing. Don't try to control your breathing. Simply observe it.

When you pay attention to the many factors that are influenced by or influence your walking action, you feel a sense of wonder for the way the human body is designed. You tend to remind yourself of the magic of nature, and how we take so many things made available to us for granted. When you walk mindfully, you are drawn to the people who are not fortunate enough to be able to walk or feel the ground beneath them. Consequently, your sense of gratitude gets a boost.

Mindful working - The modern world inventions, especially the computer, have created a misconception in our minds that multitasking is a sign of efficiency and productivity. This attitude is completely far from the truth. Multitasking is for machines, not for human beings.

So, the next time you want to do two or three tasks together, stop for a moment and recall the following disadvantages of multitasking, which is the opposite of single-tasking or working at one task mindfully.

Compromised quality of work - When your focus is shifting from one task to another, there is bound to be compromised quality. Mistakes are likely to happen in all the tasks that you are simultaneously involved in.

Chronic distraction - When your mind is filled with the thoughts of more than one task, it is likely to be distracted by a second task when you are doing the first, and vice versa. You run the risk of being continuously distracted by the thoughts of all the tasks you have undertaken in your multitasking exercise.

Sows the seeds of procrastination - When you believe that you can do more than one task at a time, you begin to postpone work because you think that you will combine what you planned for today with tomorrow's task. Therefore, multitasking sows the seeds of a procrastinating attitude.

Therefore, focus on one task at a time and make sure your body and mind are totally immersed in the job. You will find your efficiency and productivity taking a big leap forward.

Daily Stoic Affirmations and Quotes for Self-Reflection

Use the following Stoic affirmations to repeat to yourself during the morning and evening self-reflection period. Repeating a fact will help you understand the value of it, and you will see that it is increasingly easy to lead the life of a peace-loving Stoic.

Fortune, wealth, or luck cannot give us anything that we can own forever. Nothing is stable in this universe. Everything is continuously changing. - Marcus Aurelius

Our worth is defined by the element to which we devote our energy. - Marcus Aurelius

Being even-minded is the biggest virtue. - Heraclitus

The more we value those elements that are outside of our control, the less control we have. - Epictetus

The only way you can achieve peace and tranquility is by letting go of what others say, do, or think. - Marcus Aurelius

The whole of your future is uncertain. Therefore, live in the present moment. - Seneca

What you bear is not as important as how you bear it. - Seneca

Just like how a gem cannot be polished without friction, so a man cannot be polished without trials and tribulations. - Seneca

The man who is happy with the least is the most content. - Diogenes

Man can conquer the world by conquering himself - Zeno of Citium

Practice indifference towards those elements that don't make a difference. - Marcus Aurelius

Fate leads the willing and drags the unwilling. - Cleanthes

A well-grounded man does not seek outside approval. - Epictetus

The biggest law of nature is that it stops for no one. It has no end. - Ryan Holiday

The man who is caught in the anxiety of the future is a miserable man. - Seneca

A wise man is not carried away by prosperity or bogged down by poverty. Such a man is happy because he has found happiness within himself. - Seneca

I love to go and see everything in the market that I am happy without. - Seneca

Wealth is not about having numerous possessions. It is about having few wants. - Epictetus

The Power of a Stoic Diary

You already know the benefits of journaling, and how important it is for Stoics to keep a journal where they make entries each day. This section is dedicated to giving you some prompts based on which you can write in your Stoic journal.

Topics for gratitude - When you pause and reflect on the people and things you are grateful for, you learn to appreciate things in your life better. You learn to value the people in your life who are contributing to make you happy, which, in turn, helps in strengthening your relationships with them. You also learn not to take anything for granted.

Use the following prompts to make gratitude-based entries in your Stoic journal. Make sure you include everyone in your list include your spouse/partner, parents, siblings, children, and other close family members, and close friends, colleagues, team members, neighbors, and all others who have impacted your life.

- ❖ What contribution has this person made to improve your life? What knowledge, experience, or event can you give this individual partial or full credit for?
- ❖ What have I done for this person to return the favor, or what can I do for him or her?
- ❖ How does this individual affect, influence, or control my life decisions, behaviors, attitudes, and choices?
- ❖ What are the traits that I admire and wish to emulate?
- ❖ What are the traits that I developed because of this person?

Other gratitude topics that you can include in your Stoic journal are your achievements, happy events, and material things you have earned in your life. Showing gratitude for what you have done and what you have got will reduce or even eliminate the craving for something you don't have. Here are a few prompts in this regard:

- ❖ What accomplishments and achievements am I proud of?

- ❖ Why do I feel this pride in my achievements?
- ❖ What can I do to continue doing well in life?
- ❖ What are the top two cherished moments of my life? Why do I cherish them so much?
- ❖ Now, think about something in your life that you want to replace or upgrade. Suppose you want to replace your refrigerator. Ask yourself these questions?
  - ➢ Is the current one working well?
  - ➢ What is the most important thing about the current refrigeration that I appreciate?
  - ➢ Will the new/upgraded item give me sustained value?
- ❖ Look at the things that you already have. How much will you crave for them if you didn't have them?

Tips to manage negative thoughts - Negative thoughts (except when you are doing negative visualizations with a purpose) steal your mind of joy and happiness. Low-value thoughts are fertile ground for chaos and unhappiness. Therefore, managing negative thoughts before they control our life is a useful Stoic tool. Here are some points to ponder on as you make entries in your Stoic journal.

- ❖ Think of something you craved for deeply and finally bought. How did you feel about the item? Do you now think that the craving was warranted?
- ❖ Now, do you have something in mind that you are craving to own? What value will it add to your life or the lives of your loved ones? What is the loss of value if you choose not to purchase the item? Can you use the money for a better purpose than the purchase of this item that you crave?
- ❖ Recall something you have done and now regret your actions. Write yourself a note of apology explaining why you did what you did. Tell yourself how you think you could have handled the situation in a better way. Also, write a note of forgiveness to yourself.

Topics for self-improvement - Self-improvement is one of the most crucial tenets of Stoicism that every Stoic practices unfailingly. Here are some topics to make journal entries for self-improvement.

- ❖ Think of a tenet or principle that you find difficult to live by. Write down the tenet and your own interpretation of it. Create your own analogy for the tenet. Keep repeating it until the tenet becomes a habit in your life.
- ❖ Think of a role model or mentor whom you look up to. Write yourself a letter from that person's perspective, giving you advice on self-improvement.
- ❖ Go back to your teens. What are the top 4 secrets of your adult life that you want to share with your adolescent self?
- ❖ Did I lose my temper today? What triggered my anger? Could I have handled the situation in a better way?
- ❖ Did I behave against my character today? What triggered my behavior? Was it within reasonable limits? Could I have done something differently?

- ❖ What are the things I did today that resulted in wastage of time? How can I avoid such situations in the future?
- ❖ Did I miss practicing a good habit or an important step in my daily routine today? Why did it happen and what measures I can take to ensure it does not happen again?
- ❖ What was my biggest craving today? Describe your craving in detail. Did the item really call for that kind of deep craving?

Don't underestimate the immense power of journaling. The more you write down your thoughts, the clearer your thinking process becomes.

Use all the suggestions given in this chapter to start off living like a Stoic daily. You can start with one suggestion, practice it for a couple of days (or how much time you need), and then add another tip to it, and so forth. Repeat this process until you have incorporated all the suggestions that are aligned with your lifestyle from this chapter. You can start by repeating one Stoic affirmation every day and contemplate on its meaning throughout the day.

Conclusion

Practicing and living the life of a Stoic is like sweeping the floor. Just because you have swept the floor once does not mean you don't need to do it again. Sweeping the floor has to be done repeatedly to keep the floor clean. In the same way, living according to Stoicism takes continued, unending practice.

Stoicism is about taming emotions and not about eliminating them. As I have already told you, I was struggling to live in peace and find happiness despite being wealthy and having materialistic resources. Due to my lack of understanding of the human mind and the play of emotions and desires, I was giving in to everything that was happening around me.

If I saw someone doing better than me in my life, I wanted to do that. If my neighbor bought a new car, I was keen on buying a better model. If my neighbor's kids did well in school, I wanted my kids to do better. The limitless desires were killing me to the point that I was losing control of my life.

And then Stoicism came to my help. The tips and suggestions given in this book are not theoretical takeaways. I found many of them useful in my own life, and therefore, wanted to share them with others who have the same struggles as I did. So, let us look at the main takeaways from this book.

Stoicism is an age-old, time-tested philosophical school of thought that was created to help human beings live a good, virtuous, and happy life. The founder was Stoicism was Zeno of Citium who lost all his possessions and cargo when his ship was wrecked. He said that he found the joy of philosophy when he lost his possessions. The key suggestions from this book that you should start implementing right away are:

- ❖ Focus on the things that are under your control and stop fretting about things you cannot control.
- ❖ The only thing that is under your influence is your behavior and attitude. So, start focusing on that and let go of everything else.
- ❖ Always look inwards when things go wrong because all solutions to your problems are

within you. Nothing is in the external surroundings.

- ❖ Remember that nothing is permanent. Everything comes to an end and dies. Therefore, don't fear death because what comes from the primordial fire goes back to it.
- ❖ Virtue is the highest good. Everything else comes after that. If you cannot live a virtuous life, then your life is not worth living.
- ❖ Managing and controlling your emotions and emotional response are crucial elements of a Stoic life. Emotions are like the weather that keeps changing. Therefore, making decisions based on your emotions is not only foolhardy but also unsustainable.
- ❖ Mastering your mind is another critical aspect of Stoicism. The more you learn to master your mind, the more control you have of your life and life choices.
- ❖ Dealing with negative emotions like anger, grief, resentment, etc. is vital to lead a carefree, stress-free, and meaningful life.

- ❖ Running away from emotions is not emotional intelligence. Being self-aware and controlling your responses to emotions is emotional intelligence.
- ❖ The Stoic Triangle of Happiness consists of taking responsibility, living with arete, and focusing on what you can control. If you can combine these three, then you can achieve eudaimonia or a flourishing life.
- ❖ Negative visualization techniques help you mentally prepare yourself for the challenges of life. It is not a pessimistic attitude but a realistic and powerful tool designed to help you overcome obstacles and difficulties in your life.

And finally, remember that Stoic practices are to be continually implemented for successful outcomes. It is not a one-time effort that you put in and then forget about it. You must make Stoicism a way of your life if you want sustainable happiness and joy in your life.

Resources

https://en.wikipedia.org/wiki/Stoicism

https://www.njlifehacks.com/what-is-stoicism-overview-definition-10-stoic-principles/

https://donaldrobertson.name/2018/01/18/what-do-the-stoic-virtues-mean/

https://www.philosophybasics.com/branch_stoicism.html

https://www.njlifehacks.com/why-stoicism-is-relevant-today/

https://99u.adobe.com/articles/24401/a-makers-guidebook-9-stoic-principles-to-nurture-your-life-and-work

https://howtobeastoic.wordpress.com/stoicism-101/

https://en.wikipedia.org/wiki/Stoicism

https://www.google.com/search?rlz=1C5CHFA_enGB812GB812&q=stoicism+stoic+philosophers&stick=

H4sIAAAAAAAAONgFuLQz9U3MLfINlKCs7REspOt9JPzc3Pz86xS8svzyhOLUopXMUoAxXJyUpNLMvPz9AsyMnPyi_MLMlKLihexSheX5GcmZxbnKoAZCsiyABtf2l9lAAAA&sa=X&ved=2ahUKEwjz0uHc5uXhAhUVShUIHSASDBQQMSgAMCR6BAgNEAE&biw=1280&bih=603https://howtobeastoic.wordpress.com/stoicism-101/https://dailystoic.com/the-stoic-philosophers/

https://www.britannica.com/biography/Ariston-of-Chios

https://www.encyclopedia.com/humanities/encyclopedias-almanacs-transcripts-and-maps/aristo-chios-third-century-bce

https://donaldrobertson.name/2014/10/12/how-not-to-be-a-stoic/

https://www.encyclopedia.com/history/biographies/panama-history-biographies/cleanthes-assos

https://www.iep.utm.edu/chrysipp/#H1

https://www.britannica.com/biography/Diogenes-of-Babylon https://www.revolvy.com/page/Antipater-of-Tarsus?cr=1

https://www.encyclopedia.com/humanities/encyclopedias-almanacs-transcripts-and-maps/panaetius-rhodes-c-185-110-bce

http://encyclopedia.kids.net.au/page/pu/Publius_Clodius_Thrasea_Paetus

https://docs.google.com/document/d/1yDTxBlktP9qSCedrYlfd9RO3Yg7cKTwrlfO19GE3xo4/edit

https://dailystoic.com/epicureanism-stoicism/

https://academyofideas.com/2014/03/stoicism-vs-epicureanism/

https://www.psychologytoday.com/us/blog/hide-and-seek/201204/are-you-epicurean-really

https://churchofepicurus.wordpress.com/basic-principles-for-the-modern-epicurean/

https://dailystoic.com/self-awareness-and-emotional-intelligence-the-keys-to-your-best-self/

https://m.wikihow.com/Be-Stoic

https://modernstoicism.com/stoicism-and-the-art-of-archery/   https://dailystoic.com/stoicism-modernity/
https://dailystoic.com/self-awareness-and-emotional-intelligence-the-keys-to-your-best-self/

https://immoderatestoic.com/blog/2013/4/2/stoic-emotionsall-three-of-them

https://www.davidhenzel.com/the-little-book-of-stoicism-review/

https://highexistence.com/seneca-on-how-to-deal-with-anger/

https://www.njlifehacks.com/stoic-negative-visualization-become-mentally-stronger/
https://www.inc.com/amy-morin/6-ways-to-stop-worrying-about-things-you-cant-control.html
https://thriveglobal.com/stories/9-ways-to-take-responsibility-for-your-life/ https://dailystoic.com/10-insanely-useful-stoic-exercises/
https://constantrenewal.com/stoic-practices/

https://medium.com/the-mission/my-incredibly-simple-guide-to-stoicism-learn-wisdom-you-can-practically-use-67a0195298ee

https://dailystoic.com/stoicism-modernity/ https://www.inc.com/chris-dessi/how-to-get-comfortable-with-being-uncomfortable-according-to-a-green-beret.html
https://www.psychologytoday.com/intl/blog/feeling-it/201212/the-brains-ability-look-within-secret-self-

mastery https://www.njlifehacks.com/prepare-yourself-for-the-day-the-stoic-morning-routine/

https://medium.com/the-mission/marcus-aurelius-on-how-to-begin-each-day-for-optimal-sanity-9993bb0118c https://greengarageblog.org/7-pros-and-cons-of-multitasking https://www.psychologytoday.com/intl/blog/what-matters-most/201509/how-practice-mindfulness-5-tips-no-one-has-told-you https://regpaq.com/stoic-journal-topics-eca08e0b60f5

http://wisdomquotes.com/stoic-quotes/

www.ingramcontent.com/pod-product-compliance
Lightning Source LLC
Chambersburg PA
CBHW031110080526
44587CB00011B/906